Edinburgh Law Essentials

PRIVATE INTERNATIONAL LAW

D1339886

EDINBURGH LAW ESSENTIALS

Series Editor: Nicholas Grier, Edinburgh Napier University

Private International Law
David Hill

Revenue Law Essentials
William Craig

Commercial Law Essentials
Malcolm Combe

Succession Law Essentials
Frankie McCarthy

Delict Essentials
Francis McManus

Scottish Legal System Essentials
Bryan Clark and Gerard Keegan

Evidence Essentials
James Chalmers

Contract Law Essential Cases
Tikus Little

Trusts Law Essentials
John Finlay

Company Law Essentials
Josephine Bisacre and Claire McFadzean

Jurisprudence Essentials
Duncan Spiers

Legal Method Essentials
Dale McFadzean and Gareth Ryan

Human Rights Law Essentials
Valerie Finch and John McGroarty

Planning Law Essentials
Anne-Michelle Slater

Contract Law Essentials
Tikus Little

Employment Law Essentials
Jenifer Ross

International Law Essentials
John Grant

Media Law Essentials
Douglas Maule and Zhongdong Niu

Intellectual Property Law Essentials
Duncan Spiers

Family Law Essentials
Kenneth Norrie

European Law Essentials
Stephanie Switzer

Roman Law Essentials
Craig Anderson

Property Law Essentials
Duncan Spiers

Medical Law Essentials
Murray Earle

Public Law Essentials
Jean McFadden and Dale McFadzean

Scottish Administrative Law Essentials
Jean McFadden and Dale McFadzean

www.euppublishing.com/series/ele

Edinburgh Law Essentials

PRIVATE INTERNATIONAL LAW

David Hill, LL.B., LL.M., Ph.D.

Lecturer in Law,
Robert Gordon University
Aberdeen

EDINBURGH
University Press

Copyright © David Hill, 2014

Edinburgh University Press Ltd
The Tun – Holyrood Road
12 (2f) Jackson's Entry
Edinburgh EH8 8PJ
www.euppublishing.com

Typeset in Bembo by
Koinonia, Bury, and
printed and bound by
CPI Group (UK) Ltd, Croydon, CR0 4YY

A CIP record for this book is available from the British Library

ISBN 978 1 84586 129 2 (paperback)
ISBN 978 0 7486 9825 7 (webready PDF)
ISBN 978 0 7486 9826 4 (epub)

The right of David Hill to be identified as author of this work has been asserted in
accordance with the Copyright, Designs and Patents Act 1988 and the Copyright and
Related Rights Regulations 2003 (SI No. 2498).

CONTENTS

TABLE OF CASES

TABLE OF LEGISLATION

1 INTRODUCTION

Private international law is the branch of law in each legal system that regulates cases with a foreign element. What this foreign element may be will vary but its existence is a necessary prerequisite before the rules of private international law will be engaged. Where all elements of a case are connected to Scotland then the rules of private international law will have no role to play and the case will be disposed of according to domestic Scots law. However, as soon as this foreign element does exist, whether this be as a consequence of the parties themselves or the subject matter of the dispute, the rules of private international law will become operative.

The increasing availability and ease of international travel and communication has fundamentally altered the world in which we live. Problems of private international law, once relegated to the periphery of a legal system, are now to the fore in almost every branch of private law. Overseas travel is no longer restricted to the wealthy and most individuals now visit foreign countries regularly, whether this be for purposes of business, education or pleasure. Even a relatively small business is likely to have a number of international suppliers and clients. International relationships of a personal nature, and the children thereof, are now commonplace. Should there be a contractual dispute between a company based in Scotland and a supplier based in Germany, or a breakdown of a marriage between a Scottish man and an Australian woman who live together with their children in England, the challenge for private international law is to provide a set of rules capable of doing justice in the given circumstances.

THE THREE PILLARS OF PRIVATE INTERNATIONAL LAW

Private international law has three key objectives:

(1) to set out the conditions under which a court will have jurisdiction to deal with a case containing a foreign element;

(2) once jurisdiction is confirmed, to identify the system of law that will be applied in order to resolve the dispute; and

(3) to determine the circumstances in which a foreign judgment will be recognised and, if necessary, enforced.

Jurisdiction

The first issue to be decided by the Scottish court is whether it has jurisdiction to hear a case which contains a foreign element. Jurisdiction is premised upon the court having some connection to the dispute, such as the fact that a contractual obligation was, or should have been, performed in Scotland, or the fact that spouses lived together as man and wife in Scotland. In a purely domestic case there will be only one appropriate forum but when a foreign element exists the rules of private international law attempt to achieve justice by delimiting the jurisdiction of the Scottish courts in order to avoid conflicts of jurisdiction with the courts of other countries. Accordingly, the Scottish jurisdictional rules identify the circumstances in which it is considered legitimate for a Scottish court to take jurisdiction over a case, even though the case has connections to a foreign country, or even a number of foreign countries. Further, as it is inevitable that in certain circumstances the same or similar proceedings may be continuing in the courts of two different countries in parallel, the rules of jurisdiction also determine what effect such foreign proceedings will have on the Scottish proceedings. As we shall see in later chapters, there are two distinct approaches to the problem of parallel proceedings: a flexible approach that originally developed in Scotland, and a more rigid approach adopted in EU legislative instruments. Finally, it is also possible for parties to clothe the courts of a particular country with jurisdiction via agreement. In certain contexts, primarily in relation to civil and commercial matters, this right of party autonomy is generally unfettered and parties are able to choose the courts of any country, whether or not that country has an objective link to the dispute. In other contexts, such as where one party is considered to be in a "weaker" position, or due to the specific nature of the dispute, the choice may be confined to a limited number of pre-established jurisdictions.

Choice of law

Once the jurisdiction of the court has been established, the rules of private international law then operate to identify the law which the court should apply in order to determine the dispute before it. As with jurisdiction, the principal concern of the choice of law rules is to identify an applicable law which is connected to the dispute and is considered to be the law most appropriate to determine the rights of the parties. As we shall see, just because a Scottish court is able to claim jurisdiction, this does not necessarily mean that Scots law will be the most appropriate law. Instead, the Scottish court will, where appropriate, apply foreign rules of law in order to determine the dispute before it. If this were not the case and the Scottish court, along with its foreign counterparts, always applied its own law in every case before it, this would lead to the problem of "forum shopping" in which a pursuer shops around the available forums in order to find the legal system most favourable to his case. Only by being open to the application of foreign rules of law can the problem of forum shopping be minimised, if not entirely prevented, and significant steps have been taken, particularly within the European Union, to ensure that, no matter where a case is brought, the same applicable law will be identified. Finally, and reflective of the approach taken towards questions of jurisdiction, it may also be possible for parties to come to an agreement as to the law to be applied to determine their dispute.

Recognition and enforcement

Issues of jurisdiction and choice of law arise when the Scottish court is asked to consider an ongoing dispute. In contrast, questions of recognition and enforcement occur when a foreign court has previously considered itself to have jurisdiction over a case, has decided that case according to the law it considered appropriate to determine the rights of the parties, and the successful party subsequently wishes to have the foreign judgment recognised and enforced in Scotland. The recognition and enforcement of foreign judgments is essential if parties are to be treated justly and fairly, as to refuse to recognise foreign judgments would force the successful party to go to the expense and inconvenience of beginning fresh proceedings in Scotland (and any other country in which they wished to have the judgment recognised and enforced). Significant steps have been taken within the European Union to facilitate the free movement of judgments by ensuring the almost automatic recognition of a judgment granted in one Member State in all other Member States, and these developments will be considered further in the relevant chapters.

THE NAME OF THE SUBJECT

The subject is variously known as "private international law", "international private law" and "the conflict of laws". This is merely a difference of nomenclature and, however described, the core of the subject is that it is the branch of law which seeks to regulate the international relations of private individuals. This can be contrasted with the subject of public international law which seeks to regulate relations between states. As regards the third formulation, it should be noted that it is not the laws themselves which will be in conflict. Indeed, one of the principal aims of the subject is to avoid such conflicts. Instead, the conflict is to be found as between the individual litigants who will have conflicting views as to the most appropriate law to be applied in the case. It is the first of these terms, "private international law", that will be utilised throughout this book.

THE MEANING OF "COUNTRY"

Already in this introduction, and many more times throughout this book, reference will be made to "foreign" courts and "foreign" laws, or the fact that elements of a particular dispute are located "overseas" in another "country". This reference to a foreign country should not be read in the political sense and, instead, a "country" for the purposes of private international law denotes any territorial unit with a separate system of law. Consequently, the United States of America is not a "country" for the purposes of private international law and reference is instead made to its constituent parts, such as the states of New York or Texas. Similarly, Scotland is a separate "country" for the purposes of private international law and the other component parts of the United Kingdom are as much a foreign country as, say, France or Germany. In light of this, the issue of "intra-UK" conflicts will be considered at various points throughout this book, although, it must be admitted, there is a large degree of similarity among the rules of private international law adopted in each part of the United Kingdom.

HARMONISATION

There has been a significant trend in recent years towards the harmonisation of the rules of private international law. While the extent of harmonisation varies, there are now certain areas in which a number of states, particularly the EU Member States, adopt harmonised rules of jurisdiction, choice of law and recognition and enforcement. Such rules ensure that the courts of different countries assume jurisdiction on identical grounds and, once jurisdiction is assumed, apply the same law to determine the relevant issues. This unified approach then facilitates the recognition and enforcement elsewhere of the resultant judgments. The majority of topics considered in this book have been subject to at least some degree of harmonisation, with such developments emanating from two principal sources.

The Hague Conference on Private International Law

The Hague Conference on Private International Law is a global inter-governmental organisation, founded in 1893, which has developed a number of multilateral legal instruments, some having met with notably more success than others. The Conference boasts a current membership of 77 members (76 states and the European Union) and a number of non-member states are also party to various conventions. Arguably the Conference's most successful instrument has been the Convention of 25 October 1980 on the Civil Aspects of International Child Abduction which will be considered in Chapter 11.

The European Union

Of increasing importance at the regional European level are the measures adopted by the European Union. Such developments have a relatively recent history, with a key change occurring on 1 May 1999 following the entry into force of the Treaty of Amsterdam, Art 65 of which empowered the EU to take measures in the field of judicial co-operation in civil matters having cross-border implications, in so far as necessary for the proper functioning of the internal market. This power was extended further with the entry into force of the Treaty of Lisbon on 1 December 2009. The Treaty of Lisbon amended the EU's two core treaties: the Treaty on European Union (TEU) and the Treaty establishing the European Community (TEC), with the latter being re-named the Treaty on the Functioning of the European Union (TFEU). Article 81 of the TFEU removed the requirement that measures on judicial co-operation in civil matters having cross-border implications be "necessary" for the proper functioning of the internal market and replaced this with the more permissive phrase that the EU adopt such measures "*particularly* when necessary for the proper functioning of the internal market" (emphasis added).

A variety of instruments have been introduced as a result of these powers, some of which have their origins prior to the entry into force of the Treaty of Amsterdam. A number of these developments will be considered throughout this book, particularly the Brussels I Regulation (Chapters 3 and 4), the Brussels IIa Regulation (Chapters 8 and 11), the Rome I Regulation (Chapter 5) and the Rome II Regulation (Chapter 6). As the United Kingdom has reserved the right to decide on a case-by-case basis whether it will participate in any particular instrument there are also a number of initiatives, such as the Rome III Regulation, to which the United Kingdom is not party.

Essential Facts

- Private international law is the branch of law in each legal system that regulates cases with a foreign element.
- Private international law has three main objectives: (1) to determine jurisdiction; (2) to identify the applicable law; and (3) to facilitate the recognition and enforcement of foreign judgments.
- There has been a significant trend in recent years towards the harmonisation of private international law, principally as a result of the work of the Hague Conference on Private International Law and the European Union.

2 PERSONAL CONNECTING FACTORS

As a consequence of the growing ease and availability of international travel, it is becoming increasingly common for individuals to develop connections with a number of legal systems during the course of their lives. At the same time, there is also an expectation that, regardless of where a person may happen to be at any given point, certain legal matters – primarily issues of legitimacy, adoption, marital status and succession – should always be governed by the law to which that person "belongs". This is known as the doctrine of personal law: a doctrine which seeks to identify the most appropriate law to deal with issues of status, regardless of the fact that the individual in question (the *propositus*) may have links (perhaps very strong links) to other systems of law.

While there is broad agreement that an individual should be "connected" to a particular law, there is less agreement regarding precisely how this connection should be established. The traditional connecting factor adopted in Scotland and almost all common-law countries is that of domicile, while most of the civil-law jurisdictions of continental Europe opt instead for the law of an individual's nationality. Both these traditional connecting factors are gradually being marginalised by the rise to prominence of the contemporary connecting factor of habitual residence.

DOMICILE

Domicile is the tie or connection between an individual and a place governed by a single system of law. Because domicile denotes a connection between an individual and a single system of law it follows that there is no such thing as a British domicile – only a Scottish domicile, an English domicile etc. Domicile is a personal matter that can be changed without state authorisation, and even without an individual realising that such a change has occurred. Accordingly, there is no "register" of domicile and any disputes as to a person's domicile can be resolved only following adjudication by the court.

The central principle underlying the concept of domicile is the identification of a person's permanent home. When international mobility was rare and the large majority of people would be born, would live and would ultimately die in the same country, often without ever leaving its confines, domicile was a relatively simple and straightforward concept. Now, however, to equate the concepts of home and domicile is too simplistic due to the attribution of the latter being subject to a number of strict legal rule – rules which can appear to pay little attention to the factual realities of a person's life. In conjunction with the sharp increase in international mobility, these strict legal rules have led to a wide gulf developing between the common-sense understanding of a person's home and the legal concept of domicile – a gulf exacerbated by the failure of numerous attempts at fundamental reform of the concept. Indeed, as will be identified below, it is perfectly possible for an individual to be domiciled in a country he has never visited. Further complexity is apparent in Scotland following the partial reform of the law as a result of s 22 of the Family Law (Scotland) Act 2006.

General principles

There are three general principles that underpin the law of domicile and influence the more detailed rules considered below:

(1) *Every individual must have a domicile.* An individual will be attributed a domicile from the moment he is born to the moment he dies and, while this domicile may change, there can be no gaps in an individual's domicile. An individual will therefore be ascribed a domicile even if the circumstances of his life suggest that he does not have a readily identifiable home.

(2) *Every individual must have only one domicile at any given time.* Even if the reality of an individual's life would suggest that he has two homes in two different countries the law of domicile refuses to countenance the idea of concurrent domiciles.

(3) *An existing domicile is presumed to continue until a new domicile has been acquired.* The burden of proving a change of domicile lies on those who assert such a change.

Domicile of a newborn – domicile of origin

In light of the fact that no person can be without a domicile, every individual will be allocated a domicile – known as a domicile of origin – from the moment of his birth. While it will often be the case that the domicile of origin will equate with the country of birth, this is entirely coincidental as the place of birth is in no way determinative of the domicile of origin. The principles of the concept of the domicile of origin were most famously set out in a Scottish appeal to the House of Lords, *Udny* v *Udny* (1869), with the decision in *Re Fuld's Estate No. 3* (1968) offering a more recent discussion of the core principles of the concept. Due to the partial reform introduced by the Family Law (Scotland) Act 2006 it is necessary to consider the law both pre- and post-4 May 2006.

The common law

Attribution of a domicile of origin under the common law was built upon the concept of legitimacy in that a legitimate child would take the domicile of his father and an illegitimate child the domicile of his mother (*Udny* v *Udny* (1869)). It is important to note that the consequence of this rule is that the domicile of origin may not necessarily reflect the factual reality of a child's life and may instead allocate a domicile in a country the child had never visited. For example, a child born in France to parents domiciled in Scotland will be assigned a Scottish domicile and a child born in Scotland to parents domiciled in France will be assigned a French domicile. Rules of varying clarity also exist in reference to the less common situations of post-humous children, children legitimated *per subsequens matrimonium*, children of putative marriages, foundlings and adopted children.

Family Law (Scotland) Act 2006

One of the aims of the 2006 Act was to effect the abolition of the status of illegitimacy, and any aspect of differential treatment predicated upon the distinction between legitimate and illegitimate children, from Scots law. This was achieved via s 21 of the Act and, as this abolition made the common-law rules regarding the attribution of a domicile of origin unworkable, s 22 introduced replacement provisions. Although this section makes no explicit reference to the concept of the domicile of origin, the fact that it applies to all persons under 16 implies that the rules contained therein are intended to apply to this initial determination of domicile. Section 22 states that:

> "(1) Subsection (2) applies where—
> (a) the parents of a child are domiciled in the same country as each other; and
> (b) the child has a home with a parent or a home (or homes) with both of them.
> (2) The child shall be domiciled in the same country as the child's parents.
> (3) Where subsection (2) does not apply, the child shall be domiciled in the country with which the child has for the time being the closest connection.
> (4) In this section, 'child' means a person under 16 years of age."

This section thus introduces two rules – one of dependence and one of independence – the applicability of which depend upon the circumstances of the child. First, the rule of dependence in s 22(2) states that where the parents are domiciled in the same country and the child has a home with one or both then the child shall be domiciled in the same country as the parents. It is important to note that the domicile of the parents and the place where the child has his home with at least one of them need not coincide for this rule to be applicable. For example, if a couple domiciled in the US state of Texas are posted to Aberdeen for a 2-year work placement and have a child while living in Scotland then the requirements of s 22(2) will be fulfilled and the child will take the parents' joint Texan domicile as his domicile of origin, regardless of the fact that the family home is currently in Scotland. Further, there is no precise definition of what constitutes a "home" for the purposes of this section. While the most common example would be where the child actually lives with one or both parents on a day-to-day basis, it is submitted that the child would still be considered as having a home with his parent(s) notwithstanding occasional absences.

If the rule of dependence does not apply, whether because the parents do not share a common domicile or, more unusually, the child does not have a home with either of them, then recourse must be had to the independent rule of s 22(3) which provides that the child will be domiciled in the country with which he has the closest connection for the time being. No guidance is given in relation to how the "closest connection" of the child is to be determined and while this may be a relatively straightforward test to apply to older children, difficulties arise when attempting to identify the country to which a newborn baby has the closest connection. If the test were to be applied literally, this would mandate an approach whereby all children were ascribed a domicile of origin in their country of birth. In the majority of cases the place of birth will be a country with which the child will go on to develop more meaningful ties and the rule will be uncontroversial. For example, a child who is born to an Anglo–Scottish couple who have lived together in Scotland for 10 years, and intend to remain in that country at least for the short term, will be ascribed a Scottish domicile of origin as Scotland is clearly the country of closest connection. However, there will also be instances in which the place of birth will be in a country in which the parent(s) either did not intend to remain or intended to remain only for a limited period. For example, a child could be born prematurely to the above Anglo–Scottish couple when they are on an overseas vacation. Alternatively, this couple could be living in a foreign country for the purposes of work when the child is born but always intend to return to Scotland. In both these scenarios an interpretation of the "closest connection" rule as a "place of birth" rule would result in the child acquiring a domicile of origin different to that of his parents and in a country with which he has only a fortuitous connection. In such circumstances an argument could be made that reference should be had to the long-term intentions of the parent(s) but this has the disadvantage that the child will then be domiciled in a country in which he has never lived, and in which he may not live for perhaps a number of years, if ever.

Transitional arrangements

Article 4 of the Family Law (Scotland) Act 2006 (Commencement, Transitional Provisions and Savings) Order 2006 (SSI 2006/212) makes it clear that the rules contained in s 22 are to apply only in relation to proceedings which commence on or after 4 May 2006. This date is also the effective date from which s 1 of the Law Reform (Parent and Child) (Scotland) Act 1986 provides that no person whose status is governed by Scots law shall be illegitimate, and the fact that a person's parents are not or have not been married to each other shall be left out of account in determining that person's legal status. It is therefore clear that any question that may arise regarding the domicile of a person under 16 who was born on or after 4 May 2006 will be determined according to s 22. There is a lack of clarity, however, regarding the law to be applied if a court is asked to determine the domicile of an individual before this date: should the common law that was then in force apply or should domicile be determined according to the now in force Family Law (Scotland) Act 2006?

This point is not addressed in the legislation and is yet to be tested by the courts but academic opinion suggests that the new domicile rules of s 22 should be applied retrospectively in any situation where it is necessary to determine such an individual's domicile on or after 4 May 2006. This approach could result in an individual being attributed a different domicile of origin to that previously identified under the common-law rules. In contrast, in circumstances where the domicile of an individual prior to the coming into force of the Act is at issue, with this determination unconnected to any finding of domicile after 4 May 2006, it has been argued that the common-law rules should continue to apply as this determination will relate exclusively to a time which precedes the abolition of illegitimacy and the introduction of s 22.

Domicile of children

Whether under the common law or the Family Law (Scotland) Act 2006 a domicile of origin will be attributed to every person at the moment they are born. This domicile will crystallise at the date of birth and any subsequent changes in the life of the individual will have no effect on the domicile of origin (this is subject to one exception in that the subsequent adoption of a child may result in a change in a domicile of origin (Adoption and Children (Scotland) Act 2007, s 40)). While it cannot be changed, a domicile of origin can, however, be displaced via the acquisition of a different domicile. The rules governing displacement and acquisition vary on the basis of, first, whether the individual in question has reached the age of 16 and, second, if the individual is under 16, whether the rules of the common law or s 22 of the 2006 Act are to be applied. We will first consider the rules applicable to persons under 16.

The common law – domicile of dependence

Under the common-law rules, a child was treated as a dependent person who was incapable of acquiring an independent domicile through his own acts. Instead, a domicile of origin of a child would only be displaced should there be a change in the domicile of the appropriate parent – the father in the case of a legitimate child or the mother in the case of an illegitimate child. This basic rule was buttressed by the more fact-specific rules contained in the Domicile and Matrimonial Proceedings Act 1973, s 4. This section has now been repealed in Scotland but remains applicable in England and Wales and Northern Ireland.

Family Law (Scotland) Act 2006

Section 22 applies to any determination of domicile between birth and the age of 16. Accordingly, a domicile of origin will be displaced whenever the circumstances of the child's life lead to a re-evaluation of domicile under either the dependent or the independent rule. For example, a domicile of origin attributed under s 22(2) will change to a domicile of dependence if the parents acquire a new shared domicile and the child has a home with at least one of them. Alternatively, if the parents of a child cease to share the same domicile, the domicile of that child will no longer be determined by s 22(2) and reference will instead be made to s 22(3) which may result in the child acquiring a new independent domicile.

Domicile of adults – domicile of choice

From the above discussion it will be apparent that the majority of children will be allocated a domicile that is dependent on either one parent (if domicile is to be determined under the common law) or both parents (if s 22(2) of the 2006 Act is applicable). Once a person reaches the age of 16 this pre-existing domicile (whether a domicile of origin, a dependent domicile or an independent domicile) will continue until it is replaced by a domicile of choice. A domicile of choice has been described as "a conclusion or inference which the law derives from the fact of a man fixing voluntarily his sole or chief residence in a particular place, with an intention of continuing to reside there for an unlimited time" (*Udny* v *Udny* (1869), per Lord Westbury at 99). Any individual with legal capacity can thus acquire a domicile of choice in a country via a combination of:

- actual physical residence in the country of choice; and
- an intent to remain in the chosen country indefinitely.

One of these factors is insufficient to facilitate a change of domicile and both must co-exist before a domicile of choice will be acquired.

Residence

Actual physical residence in a country is fundamental to the acquisition of a domicile of choice. In the absence of residence no amount of intention will suffice and an individual cannot acquire a domicile of choice by wishful thinking alone (*Willar* v *Willar* (1954), per Lord Justice-Clerk Thomson at 147). Conversely, the fact of actual residence, even for a number of decades, will be insufficient if there is a lack of the requisite level of intent. For example, in *Ramsay* v *Liverpool Royal Infirmary* (1930) the House of Lords held, in the absence of adequate proof as regards intent, that a man who had lived in England for 37 years had not acquired a domicile of choice in that jurisdiction. Once actual residence is coupled with the requisite level of intent then the duration of the residence will not be relevant. Thus, residence for even a very short period of time will be sufficient for the acquisition of a domicile of choice if evidence of an intent to remain in the chosen country indefinitely is available.

Intention

A domicile of choice will be acquired only if an individual has the intention to reside permanently, or for an unlimited time, in a particular country. The residence must be "freely chosen, and not prescribed or dictated by any external necessity, such as the duties of office, the demands of creditors, or the relief from illness" (*Udny* v *Udny* (1869), per Lord Westbury at 99). Doubts as to long-term intentions or lingering wishes in the mind of the individual to live elsewhere will also be fatal to the acquisition of a domicile of choice, irrespective of the length of actual residence. In contrast, residence that at its inception is "prescribed or dictated" may ultimately lead to a change of domicile if that residence later becomes voluntary. In *Mark* v *Mark* (2005) the House of Lords held that, although it is a relevant factor, the mere fact that residence in a country is unlawful does not automatically preclude the acquisition of a domicile therein.

When attempting to identify the requisite level of intent there is "no act, no circumstance in a man's life, however trivial it may be in itself, which ought to be left out of consideration" (*Drevon* v *Drevon* (1864), per Kindersley VC at 133). All evidence as to intent will be considered and there is no single factor which is automatically determinative of domicile. Further, a factor which is treated as decisive in one case may be disregarded in another. Thus, while evidence that an individual has clearly made his home for a very long time in a country, as well as having his family in that country and having no home elsewhere, is a "strong starting point", it may not be conclusive (*Holliday* v *Musa* (2010), per Waller LJ at [67]). Declarations as to intent may be relevant but such evidence, if available, is to be treated with caution and viewed in light of the speaker's motives. It is important that any such declarations are consistent with the speaker's other statements and actions (*Ross* v *Ross* (1930)). The nature of an individual's residence can also provide evidence of intent, with the purchase of a house arguably providing a stronger argument in favour of permanent intent than, say, living in rental accommodation or in a hotel.

Loss of a domicile of choice

Once acquired, a domicile of choice in a country can only be abandoned when an individual both ceases to reside physically and ceases to intend to reside permanently or indefinitely in that country. If one of these elements remains, ie an individual decides that he no longer wishes to reside in a country permanently but he does not physically leave, a domicile of choice will continue. While the departure from a country with the positive intention not to return will lead to the immediate loss of a domicile of choice, it is also possible for a domicile to be lost with a less forthright mentality by which a "withering away" of intention occurs over time (*Morgan* v *Cilento* (2004)). When a domicile of choice is abandoned it is lost forever and can only be re-acquired via a fresh concurrence of physical residence and an intent to remain permanently in the country in question.

It will often be the case that a termination of both residence and the intent to remain permanently in one country will be followed immediately by the beginning of residence with an intent to remain permanently in another country. In such circumstances the previous domicile of choice will be replaced by a new domicile of choice. An individual may, however, leave one country with the positive intent not to return but not immediately settle elsewhere, therefore losing a previous domicile of choice without acquiring a new domicile. As a fundamental principle of the law of domicile is that an individual must never be without a domicile, in these circumstances the domicile of origin is deemed to revive. This rule was detailed in *Udny* v *Udny* (1869), where Lord Westbury explained that revival was possible because the domicile of origin was never truly lost:

> "When another domicil is put on, the domicil of origin is for that purpose relinquished, and remains in abeyance during the continuance of the domicil … It revives and exists wherever there is no other domicil, and it does not require to be regained or reconstituted animo et facto in the manner which is necessary for the acquisition of a new domicil of choice." (at 99)

The domicile of origin will revive even if the individual concerned has not returned to that particular country. Indeed, the domicile of origin will revive even if, as is possible under both the common law and the Family Law (Scotland) Act 2006, the individual concerned has never been to this country or had only a transient and long-forgotten connection to this place. The revival doctrine has been criticised for potentially leading to artificial and absurd results and it has been rejected in other countries in favour of a rule of continuance, ie in similar circumstances a previous domicile of choice will continue to apply until a new one is required. This approach, while perhaps superficially superior, is also open to criticism as it may still lead to the application of an inappropriate law in that it mandates a continuing connection to a country that the individual has severed all ties with. A hybrid approach was suggested in the Court of Queen's Bench of Alberta where it was held that, while the revival rule should normally be followed, if this approach produced an absurd result (such as where the revived domicile of origin had absolutely no relevance to an individual's life, home, and activities) then a common-law judge had a residual authority to instead conclude that the individual has retained his last domicile of choice (*Re Foote Estate* (2009)).

NATIONALITY

Although the United Kingdom, and many other countries, traditionally rely upon the connecting factor of domicile, other countries utilise the concept of nationality in order to connect an individual to a particular legal system. In comparison with domicile, the main advantage that the use of nationality as a connecting factor provides is that it is much more easily ascertained, and therefore more certain. Whereas an individual may be unsure as to his domicile, he will more than likely be aware of his nationality and have documentary evidence to prove it in the form of a passport. On the other hand, this one advantage is outweighed by a number of serious disadvantages. First, as with domicile, reliance upon nationality may identify a law with which the person in question no longer has any real connection. Second, whereas an individual may have only one domicile, the possibility of dual nationality causes difficulties when attempting to connect an individual to a single legal system. In contrast, the problem of statelessness means that a person may not be connected to any legal system if nationality were the chosen connecting factor. Third, nationality cannot be utilised as a connecting factor in composite states such as the United Kingdom which are made up of a number of separate legal systems.

HABITUAL RESIDENCE

In comparison with domicile, habitual residence is intended to be a factual concept unblemished by the artificial legal rules which have come to characterise the former. Reliance on the concept of habitual residence has developed in recent times principally as a result of its utilisation by the Hague Conference on Private International Law, most notably in the Convention of 25 October 1980 on the Civil Aspects of International Child Abduction. Further, its adoption by the European Union as the primary connecting factor in a number of private international law instruments has confirmed its position as the connecting factor of choice in a number of legal spheres.

There is no single accepted definition of the concept, with a policy decision taken not to provide such a definition in order to leave habitual residence free from the rigid legal rules that have so bedevilled the determination of domicile. Instead, habitual residence is intended to be a connecting factor that reflects the factual reality of an individual's life in identifying his current centre of gravity – something that will not always be possible with domicile. This very broad statement does, however, hide a number of complexities. First, while there may be no accepted definition of the concept, a significant body of case law has developed in which habitual residence has been considered and this has inevitably led to an entrenchment upon the purely factual nature of the concept. Second, the meaning of "habitual residence" may differ according to the circumstances in which it is applied, with there being two distinct interpretations of the concept – one developed domestically and the other developed through EU legislation. Moreover, within each of these two broad interpretations further variation is possible, as the meaning of "habitual residence" may differ depending on the precise statutory context.

General characteristics

Although there is no settled definition of habitual residence, judicial consideration of the concept has led to a number of general rules and characteristics being developed. It must be remembered, however, that these are not absolutes, and what is applicable in one specific context might be inapplicable in another. With that caveat in mind, the following characteristics may be identified:

- *Habitual residence may be equated with ordinary residence.* It has been stated in the House of Lords that habitual residence is interchangeable with the older concept of ordinary residence (*Mark* v *Mark* (2005)). Exact equivalence will, however, depend on the context in which the respective concepts are used.
- *Habitual residence may be lost in a day.* A person can cease to be habitually resident in a country in a single day if he leaves that country with a settled intention not to return (*Al Habtoor* v *Fotheringham* (2001)).
- *Habitual residence cannot be acquired in a day.* An individual cannot become habitually resident in a country in a single day. Instead, an appreciable period of time and a settled intention will be necessary for the acquisition of a habitual residence (*Re J (A Minor) (Abduction: Custody Rights)* (1990)). This may be subject to exceptions where it is necessary for an individual to have a habitual residence for the purpose of making a particular piece of legislation work, or where an individual is returning to a previous habitual residence (*Nessa* v *Chief Adjudication Officer* (1999)).
- *An individual may be without a habitual residence.* As a corollary of the previous two points, it is possible for an individual to be without a habitual residence at certain points in his life.
- *Residence may become habitual whether it is involuntary or illegal.* In comparison with domicile, habitual residence may be acquired involuntarily, as a moment will come when the length of time spent in a country will override any intention not to acquire an attachment thereto (*Cameron* v *Cameron* (1996)). In *Mark* v *Mark* (2005) the House of Lords held that residence in England need not be lawful for the purpose of establishing divorce jurisdiction.
- *An individual may have more than one habitual residence.* While there is a desire in child abduction case law to avoid a finding of multiple habitual residences, the English Court of Appeal has been prepared

to accept the existence of dual habitual residences in the context of divorce jurisdiction (*Ikimi* v *Ikimi (Divorce: Habitual Residence)* (2001)).

Acquisition and loss

In *Re J (A Minor) (Abduction: Custody Rights)* (1990), Lord Brandon stated (at 578-579) that the acquisition of a habitual residence required both residence in a country for an appreciable period of time along with a settled intention to remain in that country. These two requirements appear ostensibly similar to those relevant to the acquisition of a domicile of choice in that there is a requirement of actual residence coupled with intent but their interpretation in relation to habitual residence differs in three fundamental ways from that applicable to domicile:

(1) Where residence has persisted for an extended period of time, evidence of a settled intent will no longer be essential for the acquisition of a habitual residence. This can be contrasted with domicile where residence for decades will not, by itself, be sufficient unless coupled with the necessary intent.

(2) In cases where the residence is short and it is therefore necessary to consider the intentions of the individual, what is required is not an intention to remain indefinitely but an intention to remain for a settled purpose with a sufficient degree of continuity (*R* v *Barnet LBC, Ex p Shah* (1983)). This requirement may be satisfied even when the intention to reside is only for a limited period (*Moran* v *Moran* (1997)).

(3) While domicile may be acquired immediately if the requisite intention exists, habitual residence requires residence for an appreciable period of time and may not be acquired in a single day. What constitutes an "appreciable period of time" will depend on the facts of the individual case and may vary from a very short period where there is clear evidence of intent, a matter of months where this is an element of doubt, to a period of years in cases where the residence is involuntary.

Habitual residence will be lost immediately if an individual leaves a country with the intention never to return. On the other hand, short-term, temporary absences will not lead to a loss of habitual residence. As the majority of cases fall somewhere between these two extremes, such as where a person moves to another country on a trial basis or for limited purposes, it will be necessary to look at the specific circumstances of the move in order to establish whether an existing habitual residence has been lost, and whether or not it has been replaced with a new habitual residence. Factors relevant in this determination include the maintenance of ties with the previous country of residence; the duration of residence in the new country; and the overall nature of the move. Even if there is clear evidence that an individual does intend to return to his country of habitual residence, through the passage of time there will come a point when the preservation of an existing habitual residence would contravene the factual nature of the concept.

Problems arise when considering the habitual residence of a child in that it may be difficult, if not impossible, to identify the necessary settled intent or purpose required for the acquisition of habitual residence in circumstances where the actual period of residence is relatively short. The approach of the courts in the United Kingdom has been to address this *lacuna* by looking instead to the intentions of the parents. Where a shared parental intention exists and this correlates with the factual reality of the child's life then the determination will be straightforward. However, in cases where there is no shared intent and the circumstances of a move are disputed the court will have to make a decision as to habitual residence in light of the character, purpose and duration of the move, with the latter factor of particular importance.

Habitual residence in the European Union

The connecting factor of habitual residence has been widely adopted by the EU legislator in a myriad of different contexts and while the concept is to be given an autonomous meaning across all Member States in each context in which it is utilised, this meaning will be influenced by the policy considerations underpinning the instrument in which it is employed and may therefore vary. In the context of the Brussels IIa Regulation (discussed in Chapter 8), the ECJ has held in both Proceedings Brought by A (2010) and *Mercredi* v *Chaffe* (2012) that the habitual residence of a child should reflect some degree of integration by the child in a social and family environment. Although the EU interpretation of habitual residence shares some common characteristics with the domestic interpretation considered above, two key differences are immediately apparent:

- *Habitual residence may be acquired immediately*. In *Swaddling* v *Adjudication Officer* (1999) the European Court of Justice established that for the purposes of social security law a person could acquire a habitual residence immediately, at least when moving from one Member State to another. The Family Division of the High Court of England and Wales has held that immediate acquisition of a habitual residence is also possible in the context of divorce jurisdiction (*Marinos* v *Marinos* (2007)).

- *An individual may have only one habitual residence.* While English domestic law recognises that an individual could be habitually resident in two different countries at the same time for the purposes of divorce jurisdiction (*Ikimi* v *Ikimi (Divorce: Habitual Residence)* (2001)), the court in *Marinos* held that the concept of habitual residence under the Brussels IIa Regulation has an autonomous meaning in Community law which required that an individual have only one habitual residence.

Essential Facts

Domicile
- An individual must always have a domicile and may have only one domicile at any given time.
- A domicile of origin will be allocated at birth and will be determined according to either the common-law rule based on legitimacy or one of the two rules contained in s 22 of the Family Law (Scotland) Act 2006.
- The domicile of an individual under the age of 16 will be determined according to either the common-law rule of dependence or one of the two rules contained in s 22 of the Family Law (Scotland) Act 2006.
- An adult will acquire a domicile of choice via a combination of actual physical residence in a country and an intent to remain in that country permanently.
- A domicile of origin will revive in circumstances where an individual abandons an existing domicile of choice without acquiring a new one.

Habitual residence
- Habitual residence is a factual concept which has been left undefined and its meaning may differ according to the context in which it is utilised.
- An individual may be without a habitual residence and in certain contexts may have more than one habitual residence.
- A habitual residence may be lost in a day but it cannot normally be acquired in a day.

- The acquisition of habitual residence requires both residence in a country for an appreciable period of time and a settled intention to remain in that country.
- Habitual residence is subject to a different interpretation when utilised in EU legislation. This interpretation is guided by the Court of Justice of the European Union.

Essential Cases

Udny v Udny (1869): a Scottish appeal to the House of Lords which sets out the principles of domicile.

Mark v Mark (2005): although it is a relevant consideration, the fact that residence is unlawful will not preclude acquisition of either domicile or habitual residence.

Re J (A Minor) (Abduction: Custody Rights) (1990): An individual cannot become habitually resident in a country in a single day. An appreciable period of time and a settled intention will be necessary for the acquisition of a habitual residence.

Swaddling v Adjudication Officer (1999): for the purposes of European Union social security legislation it is possible for an individual moving between Member States to acquire a habitual residence immediately. Proceedings Brought by A (2010): under Brussels IIa Regulation the habitual residence of a child should reflect some degree of integration by the child in a social and family environment.

3 JURISDICTION IN CIVIL AND COMMERCIAL MATTERS

The rules of jurisdiction determine whether or not a court can hear a case and this chapter considers the rules of Scots law that delimit the jurisdiction of the Scottish courts to hear actions in civil and commercial matters which contain a foreign element. The principle underpinning these rules is one of appropriateness, in that a Scottish court should only exercise jurisdiction over a dispute when it can be considered to be an appropriate forum to hear the action and dispose of the case. The requirement of appropriateness may be satisfied in a number of ways including, but not limited to: a link between at least one of the parties and the forum; a link between the subject-matter of the dispute and the forum; or the fact that the parties have agreed that a particular forum should have jurisdiction over the dispute. The importance of jurisdiction cannot be underestimated as from this will flow, among other important consequences, the power to classify the nature of the problem, the right to apply the procedural law of the forum and also the power to decide the applicable substantive law.

THE FOUR LEGISLATIVE REGIMES

Four different sets of rules are in place to govern the jurisdiction of the Scottish courts regarding civil and commercial matters. These are:

(1) The Brussels I Regulation

Council Regulation (EC) No 44/2001 of 22 December 2000 on jurisdiction and the recognition and enforcement of judgments in civil and commercial matters is the primary European legal instrument in this area. The Regulation applies in every Member State of the European Union, Denmark having accepted its terms via the Agreement between the European Community and the Kingdom of Denmark on jurisdiction and the recognition and enforcement of judgments in civil and commercial matters with effect from 1 July 2007. This Regulation replaced the Brussels Convention on Jurisdiction and the Enforcement of Judgments in Civil and Commercial Matters 1968 from 1 March 2002. As there was no fundamental change in structure or provisions as between the 1968 Brussels Convention and the Brussels I Regulation, case law decided under the former remains relevant in the interpretation of the latter. The Civil Jurisdiction and Judgments Act 1982 (CJJA 1982) gave force of law within the United Kingdom to the

1968 Brussels Convention, with this Act later amended by the Civil Jurisdiction and Judgments Order 2001 (SI 2001/3929) and the Civil Jurisdiction and Judgments Regulations (SI 2007/1655) in order to accommodate
the Regulation. The Brussels I Regulation will itself be replaced from 10
January 2015 by Regulation (EU) No 1215/2012 of the European Parliament and of the Council of 12 December 2012 on jurisdiction and the
recognition and enforcement of judgments in civil and commercial matters
(recast) and reference will be made to the key changes to be introduced by
the recast Regulation where necessary throughout this chapter. Although
the provisions of the Regulation will be considered in numerical order it
is important to note that there is a (non-numerical) hierarchical approach
taken to jurisdiction, with the exclusive jurisdictions in Art 22 at the apex,
followed by submission under Art 24, then the protective jurisdictions of
Arts 8–21, then "choice of court" agreements under Art 23 and, finally,
the general and special grounds of jurisdiction in Arts 2, 5 and 6. Each of
these grounds will be discussed in turn below.

(2) The Lugano Convention

The Lugano Convention on jurisdiction and the recognition and enforcement of judgments in civil and commercial matters was signed at Lugano on
16 September 1988. The 1988 Lugano Convention was largely modelled
on the 1968 Brussels Convention, with the object being to apply the principles of the latter as between the Member States of the European Union
and members of the European Free Trade Association (EFTA). Although
Lugano was considered to be a "parallel" Convention, there remained some
important differences between the two Conventions. The Lugano Convention was given effect in the United Kingdom by the Civil Jurisdiction and
Judgments Act 1991. The transformation of the 1968 Brussels Convention into the Brussels I Regulation led to a revision of the original Lugano
Convention, with a revised Convention agreed on 30 October 2007. The
text of the 2007 Lugano Convention is substantially identical to that of
the Brussels I Regulation and applies as between all Member States and
Norway, Switzerland and Iceland. The Civil Jurisdiction and Judgment
Regulations 2009 (SI 2009/3131) have amended the CJJA 1982 to reflect
the entry into force of the 2007 Lugano Convention. The consideration
of the provisions of the Brussels I Regulation set out below can be read as
also applying to the equivalent provisions of the 2007 Lugano Convention.

(3) CJJA 1982, Sch 4: intra-United Kingdom jurisdictional rules

Schedule 4 of the CJJA 1982 contains a modified version of the Brussels I Regulation for the purpose of allocating jurisdiction as between the

different parts of the United Kingdom. The provisions of Sch 4 generally follow those of the Regulation, although they are not absolutely identical. A brief mention is made at the end of this chapter regarding the circumstances in which the rules of Sch 4 differ from the equivalent provisions of the Brussels I Regulation.

(4) CJJA 1982, Sch 8: the residual Scottish rules

The rules in Sch 8 take effect subject to the Brussels I Regulation, the 2007 Lugano Convention and Sch 4 to the CJJA 1982. Broadly speaking, therefore, the rules of Sch 8 apply only in "non-European" cases, ie when a defender is not domiciled in an EU or EFTA Member State. The rules themselves are in some cases identical to the Regulation, in other cases similar, and in further cases remain in the form originally adopted under the 1968 Brussels Convention. Further detail regarding the rules of Sch 8 can be found in Beaumont and McEleavy, *Anton's Private International Law* (3rd edn, W Green, 2011), Chapter 8.

BRUSSELS I REGULATION

Scope

Article 1(1) provides that the Brussels I Regulation shall apply in civil and commercial matters whatever the nature of the court or tribunal. The Regulation shall not, however, extend, in particular, to revenue, customs or administrative matters. Article 1(2) states specifically that the Regulation will not apply to: (a) the status or legal capacity of natural persons, rights in property arising out of a matrimonial relationship, wills and succession; (b) bankruptcy, proceedings relating to the winding-up of insolvent companies or other legal persons, judicial arrangements, compositions and analogous proceedings; (c) social security; and (d) arbitration. Aside from the specific exclusions noted, the term "civil and commercial matters" is left undefined in the Regulation. The ECJ has held that this term must be given an autonomous meaning not tied to the understanding of any one legal system but interpreted primarily according to the objectives and scheme of the then Convention and, secondarily, to the general principles which emerge from the totality of the national legal systems (*LTU* v *Euro-control* (1976)).

The precise ambit of the arbitration exclusion under Art 1(2)(d) was considered in the *West Tankers* case (*Allianz SpA (formerly Riunione Adriatica di Sicurta SpA)* v *West Tankers Inc* (2009)). The decision of the ECJ in this case – to the effect that court proceedings incidentally related to arbitration did come within the scope of the Regulation, and could therefore oust, at least temporarily, the jurisdiction of the courts at the seat of arbitration – caused much controversy in the United Kingdom. The decision in *West Tankers* and the attendant dismay therewith is reflected in the terms of the recast Regulation which retains the arbitration exclusion in Art 1(2)(d) but introduces an explanatory recital (Recital (12)) with the effect that the decision in *West Tankers* is overturned at least to the extent that it required a court of one Member State to decline jurisdiction in deference to proceedings in another Member State apparently in breach of an arbitration agreement.

General jurisdiction

Article 2(1) of the Regulation states that persons domiciled in a Member State shall, whatever their nationality, be sued in the courts of that Member State. This is the primary jurisdictional basis contained in the Regulation, with the underlying principle being that the defendant should normally be sued in his "home" court. A person domiciled in a Member State other than the United Kingdom may be sued in Scotland only if the Scottish courts have jurisdiction as a result of one of the alternative grounds of jurisdiction found within the Regulation (Art 3).

Individuals

The discussion of personal connecting factors in the previous chapter focused on the traditional definition of domicile that is utilised to identify a long-term and enduring link between an individual and a particular legal system in matters of status. This traditional definition of domicile is considered to be somewhat cumbersome, possibly difficult to ascertain, and also possessing the potential to produce artificial results. The 1968 Brussels Convention left the definition of domicile to individual states and the United Kingdom opted to introduce a bespoke, residence-based definition of domicile more appropriate for determining jurisdiction in civil and commercial matters. The definition was introduced for the Convention in s 41 of the CJJA 1982, with the corresponding provision for the Brussels I Regulation contained in the Civil Jurisdiction and Judgments Order 2001, Sch 1, para 9.

The rules provide that an individual will be domiciled in the United Kingdom if and only if he is resident in the United Kingdom and the nature and circumstances of this residence indicate that he has a substantial connection with the United Kingdom (Sch. 1, para 9(2)). An identical rule applies to the identification of domicile within a particular part of the United Kingdom (para 9(3)) with an individual further considered to be domiciled in a particular place of the particular part if he has a substantial connection to the latter and is resident in the former (para 9(4)). The term "substantial connection" is left undefined but will be presumed to be fulfilled when an individual has been resident in the United Kingdom, or part thereof, for the last 3 months or more (para 9(6)). This presumption will apply unless the contrary is proven. Paragraph 9(5) addresses the situation where an individual is considered to be domiciled in the United Kingdom but lacks a substantial connection to any particular part, by stating that he is to be treated as domiciled in the part of the United Kingdom in which he is resident. Continuous residence for the entire 3-month period is not a prerequisite for the acquisition of domicile and, in contrast to the traditional understanding of domicile, it is possible for an individual to have more than one domicile under these provisions (*Daniel* v *Foster* (1989)).

If a Scottish court has to determine whether an individual is domiciled in another Member State then Art 59(2) requires that the court must apply the law of this other state. This contrasts with the traditional approach to domicile under which a Scottish court will apply Scots law to determine the domicile of an individual anywhere in the world. The Regulation does not address the determination of the domicile of a person in a state other than a Member State. In the United Kingdom an individual will be domiciled in a third state if he is resident in that state and the nature and circumstances of his residence indicate that he has a substantial connection with that state (para 9(7)). This is an identical test to that applied to determine domicile in the United Kingdom but one which does not utilise the presumption based on 3 months' residence.

Corporations

Unlike the position for individuals, the Brussels I Regulation does provide an autonomous definition of the domicile of corporations and other legal persons. Article 60 provides that such an entity will be domiciled at the place where it has its statutory seat, central administration or principal place of business. As the concept of "statutory seat" is unknown in the United Kingdom and Ireland, Art 60(2) provides that this phrase should be construed as meaning the registered office or, where there is no such office anywhere, the place of incorporation or, where there is no such place anywhere, the place under the law of which the formation took place. As with the position for individuals, it is possible, under the terms of Art 60, for a juristic person to have more than one domicile.

Special jurisdiction

Although primacy is given to the courts of the defender's domicile, Art 5 of the Regulation permits a claimant to pursue his claim in another forum when there is a close link between the subject-matter of the dispute and the alternative forum. The most important grounds of special jurisdiction relate to contract and delict.

Contract

Article 5(1)(a): Article 5(1)(a) of the Brussels I Regulation states that a person domiciled in a Member State may, in another Member State, be sued in matters relating to a contract, in the courts for the place of performance of the obligation in question. The characterisation of a matter as one "relating to contract" is given an autonomous definition and includes cases where one party denies that a contract exists (*Boss Group Ltd* v *Boss France SA* (1997)). The House of Lords held in *Kleinwort Benson Ltd* v *Glasgow City Council (No 2)* (1999) that an action for restitution for sums paid under a contract subsequently declared void were claims based on unjustified enrichment rather than contract and therefore did not fall within the terms of Art 5(1)(a).

Article 5(1)(a) gives jurisdiction to the courts for the place of performance of the obligation in question, meaning that obligation which forms the basis of the legal proceedings. The place of performance of other independent obligations under the contract will not be relevant in identifying this place (*De Bloos SPRL* v *Bouyer SA* (1976)). It is common for a claim to relate to several distinct contractual obligations with differing places of performance and this could cause any litigation brought under Art 5(1)(a) to become fragmented across jurisdictions. Such a separation of jurisdiction can be avoided if a principal obligation can be identified, with the courts for the place of performance of that principal obligation then having jurisdiction not only over that claim but also over all other claims in relation to obligations that are considered accessory to the principal, even if the accessory obligations have a different place of performance (*Shenavai* v *Kreischer* (1987)). However, the principal obligation must form part of the basis of proceedings (*Bitwise Ltd* v *CPS Broadcast Products BV* (2003)). If a principal obligation cannot be identified because multiple obligations are considered to be of equal importance, a court will have jurisdiction only in respect of the obligation the place of performance of which is within its territory (*Leathertex Divisione Sinetici SpA* v *Bodetex BVBA* (1999)).

Where a single place of performance cannot be identified then any reliance on Art 5(1)(a) will be frustrated. Thus, in *Besix SA* v *Wassereinigungsbau Alfred Kretzschmar GmbH & Co KG* (2003) the ECJ held that Art 5(1) of the Convention, which is in identical terms to Art 5(1)(a) of the Regulation, did not apply to a dispute relating to the breach of a worldwide exclusivity clause as by its very nature this clause could not be said to be performed solely in one place and no single place of performance was therefore identifiable.

Article 5(1)(b): Article 5(1)(b) of the Regulation was introduced in order to remedy the difficulties that had arisen under the 1968 Brussels Convention, by providing tailored rules applicable to the two most common forms of contracts, those for the sale of goods and the provision of services. Accordingly, for the purpose of this provision and unless otherwise agreed, the place of performance of the obligation in question is to be, in the case of the sale of goods, the place in a Member State where, under the contract, the goods were delivered or should have been delivered and, in the case of the provision of services, the place in a Member State where, under the contract, the services were provided or should have been provided. These provisions are to apply "unless otherwise agreed", meaning that the parties are permitted to come to an agreement concerning the place of performance. Moreover, it should be noted that Art 5(1)(b) operates to locate all obligations under a contract within a single country: either the place of delivery or the place where the services were provided. Unlike the position under Art 5(1)(a), there is no specific focus on the place of performance of the precise obligation in question. If Art 5(1)(b) does not apply then Art 5(1)(c) directs that Art 5(1)(a) should be relied on.

Problems have arisen under Art 5(1)(b) concerning the identification of the place of performance when goods are to be delivered to, or services provided in, more than one place. In the case of the sale of goods, the European Court held in *Color Drack GmbH* v *Lexx International Vertriebs GmbH* (2010) that where there are several places of delivery all within the same Member State, the principal place of delivery should be identified and, if such a place was not identifiable, the claimant could bring proceedings in the place of delivery of his choice. In *Wood Floor Solutions Andreas Domberger GmbH* v *Silva Trade SA* (2010) the European Court considered a similar issue but this time in relation to a contract for the provision of services in different Member States. The court held that the place of performance should be construed as referring to the place where the main provision of services is performed. In the present case, concerned with a commercial agency contract, the European Court added that where this place could not be identified then the place of performance would be considered to be the place of the agent's domicile. In *Rehder* v *Air Baltic Corp* (2010), where a passenger wished to claim compensation from an airline for a cancelled flight from Germany to Lithuania, the European Court held that both the place of departure and the place of arrival were equally closely linked to the contract for the provision of services and the claimant could choose to sue in either place.

Difficulties have also arisen as regards the application of Art 5(1)(b) to contracts which combine obligations for both the provision of services and for the sale of goods, with these obligations being performed in different Member States. In *Société ND Conseil SA* v *Société Le Meridien Hotels et Resorts World Headquarters* (2007) a contract concerned with the creation of advertising and promotional material, together with the manufacturing and packaging of that material in England before its delivery to the customer in France, was held by the French Cour de Cassation to be one for the provision of services, with the consequence that the place of performance under Art 5(1)(b) was England. In *Car Trim GmbH* v *KeySafety Systems Srl* (2010) the European Court held that a contract could still be classified as a contract for the sale of goods even in circumstances where the supplier is required to produce and manufacture the goods according to the specific requirements of the customer.

Delict

Article 5(3) of the Brussels I Regulation provides that a person domiciled in a Member State may, in another Member State, be sued in matters relating to tort, delict or quasi-delict in the courts for the place where the harmful event occurred or may occur. In the case of *Kalfelis* v *Bankhaus Schroder Munchmeyer Hengst & Co* (1988) the European Court declared that an autonomous meaning should be given to the phrase "matters relating to tort, delict or quasi-delict" to the effect that it covered all actions which seek to establish the liability of a defendant and which are not related to a "contract" within the meaning of Art 5(1). The court in *Kalfelis* further emphasised that any court with jurisdiction under Art 5(3) would have jurisdiction only as regards the delictual element of a claim and would not have jurisdiction with regard to any other matters not based in delict.

The European Court has also been asked to consider the meaning of the phrase "the place where the harmful event occurred or may occur" in light of multi-locality delicts, ie where elements of the delict, most obviously the place of acting and the place of effect, are located in different Member States. In *Handelswekerij GJ Bier BV* v *Mines de Potasse d'Alsace SA* (1978) the pollution of the Rhine in France harmed the plants of a market gardener in the Netherlands and the European Court held that the defender could be sued in either the courts for the place where the damage occurred (the Netherlands) or for the courts of the place of the event giving rise to this damage (France). More recently, in *Zuid-Chemie BV* v *Philippo's Mineralenfabriek NV/SA* (2009), in a case where a defective product was produced in Germany but used by the claimant in the Netherlands, the European Court held that the "place where the damage occurred" referred to the place where the damage occurred as a result of the normal use of the product for which it was intended (the Netherlands), with the place of the event giving rise to the damage being where the product was (defectively) produced (Germany).

The ruling in *Bier* has been applied to a claim of damage to reputation in the context of a multi-state defamation in the case of *Shevill* v *Presse Alliance SA* (1995). In this case the European Court held that the phrase "place where the harmful event occurred" should be interpreted as to give jurisdiction to both the courts of the place where a defamatory article was published (in this case, France) and, in addition, the courts of each country in which the publication was distributed and where damage to reputation was sustained. In *Shevill* this meant that the claimant was able to bring proceedings in England even though only 230 copies out of a total number of approximately 252,792 copies were sold within that jurisdiction. The European Court did, however, limit the effect of this decision by holding that only the courts of the place where the publisher was established could award damages for all harm sustained, wherever it occurred. In contrast, if the claim were brought in the courts of a place where the publication was distributed then the courts of that place could award damages only for the harm suffered within the chosen jurisdiction.

The decision in *Shevill* was revisited by the European Court in the context of material published online in the joined cases of *eDate Advertising GmbH* v *X and Martinez* v *MGN Ltd* (2011). In its decision the Court acknowledged that the universality of information disseminated via the internet reduces the effectiveness of distribution as a criterion for establishing jurisdiction and, consequently, the approach taken in *Shevill* required adaptation. Accordingly, the Court held that a person who considered that his personality rights had been infringed by means of content placed online on an internet website could bring an action, first, in respect of all the damage caused, before the courts of either the Member State in which the publisher of the content was established or the Member State in which the centre of his interests is based, or, second, before the courts of each Member State in the territory of which content placed online was or had been accessible, but only in respect of the damage caused in the territory of that Member State

The place where the harmful event occurred is limited to those places where direct damage is suffered and the courts of those places in which the indirect consequences of this damage are suffered, most obviously through financial losses, will not have jurisdiction under Art 5(3). Thus, in *Dumez France SA* v *Hessische Landesbank* (1990) it was held that Art 5(3) did not give the French courts jurisdiction in an action by the French parents of German subsidiary companies against German banks whose conduct had allegedly caused the German subsidiaries to become insolvent, thereby causing loss to the parent companies. Jurisdiction under Art 5(3) is thus limited to the place where the harmful event actually occurs, not the place where the claimant feels the adverse consequences of this event. This logic was applied by the English Court of Appeal in the case of *Henderson v Jaouen* (2002) in deciding that when a person who had suffered personal injuries resulting from a road accident in France experienced a deterioration of his condition in England this fact was not sufficient to clothe the English courts with jurisdiction.

Other special jurisdictions

Article 5 also provides grounds of special jurisdiction in matters relating to maintenance (Art 5(2)); as regards a civil claim for damages or restitution which is based on an act giving rise to criminal proceedings (Art 5(4)); as regards a dispute arising out of the operations of a branch, agency or other establishment (Art 5(5)); in claims against a person in their role as settlor, trustee or beneficiary of certain trusts (Art 5(6)); and as regards a dispute concerning the payment of remuneration claimed in respect of the salvage of a cargo or freight (Art 5(7)). The first of these, jurisdiction in matters relating to maintenance, has now been superseded by Council Regulation (EC) No 4/2009 of 18 December 2008 on jurisdiction, applicable law, recognition and enforcement of decisions and co-operation in matters relating to maintenance obligations (see Chapter 10) and has been removed from the recast Regulation. Article 7 provides a special ground of jurisdiction operative in actions relating to liability from the use or operation of a ship.

Co-defendants, third parties and counterclaims

Article 6 permits a person domiciled in a Member State to be sued in another Member State if he is one of a number of co-defendants, a third party in an action on warranty or guarantee, or on a counterclaim arising from the same contracts or facts on which the original claim was based. As regards the first of these grounds, where a person is one of a number of co-defendants, the claims must be so closely connected that it is expedient to hear and determine them together to avoid the risk of irreconcilable judgments resulting from separate proceedings. Claims may still be considered closely connected even if they have different legal bases (*Freeport Plc v Arnoldsson* (2008)). Proceedings may be consolidated in the domicile of the "anchor" defendant even if this person is not the "main", or most important, defendant; once the requirement of a close connection is established there is no further need to establish separately that the claims were not brought solely for the purpose of removing the main defendant from the jurisdiction of the courts of the Member State in which he is domiciled. In *Stewart* v *Trafalgar House Steamship Co Ltd* (2013) Lord Uist, sitting in the Outer House of the Court of Session, ruled that jurisdiction established under Art 6(1) on the basis of an "anchor" defendant will continue even if it is discovered subsequently that an action against this defendant was incompetent. Jurisdiction will be established at the time the action is raised and, once established, could not be lost, whatever might happen to the action.

Protective jurisdiction

The Brussels I Regulation makes special provision for the determination of jurisdiction in matters relating to insurance (Section 3, Arts 8–14), consumer contracts (Section 4, Arts 15–17) and individual contracts of employment (Section 5, Arts 18–21). These bespoke provisions are considered necessary in order to protect the perceived "weaker" party of the insured, the consumer and the employee respectively.

Matters relating to insurance

Articles 8–14 provide an almost exclusive code governing jurisdiction in matters related to insurance as between the insurer and the insured. Most notably, Art 9(1)(b) states that an insurer domiciled in a Member State may be sued in another Member State, in the case of actions brought by the policyholder, the insured or a beneficiary, in the courts for the place where the plaintiff is domiciled. The geographical reach of this provision is enlarged by the "deemed domicile" provision of Art 9(2) which states that an insurer who is not domiciled in a Member State but has a branch, agency or other establishment in one of the Member States shall, in disputes arising out of the operations of the branch, agency or establishment, be deemed to be domiciled in that Member State. The policyholder, the insured or a beneficiary – all of whom are considered to be the weaker party in matters relating to insurance – thus has the option to sue in his own domicile: a reversal of the principle underlying the general jurisdictional provision of Art 2. Articles 10 and 11(1) provide additional provisions in respect of liability insurance and the insurance of immoveable property.

Article 12(1) provides that an insurer may bring proceedings against a policyholder, the insured or a beneficiary only in the courts of the Member State in which the defendant is domiciled, subject to the exceptions contained in Arts 11(3) and 12(2). Article 13 limits the possibility of these protective rules being circumvented by a "choice of court" agreement under Art 23 (discussed below), by providing that such an agreement will be valid only if it complies with that article. Under the terms of Arts 13(5) and 14 these limitations do not apply to cases of marine, aviation and "large risks" insurance. These rules of protective jurisdiction are subject to the rule of Art 24 (discussed below) granting jurisdiction to the court of the Member State before which a defendant enters an appearance. This will continue to be the case under the terms of the recast Regulation but the new Art 26 thereof will require that where the policyholder, the insured or a beneficiary does enter an appearance the court shall ensure that the defendant is informed of his right to contest the jurisdiction of the court and of the consequences of entering an appearance.

Consumer contracts

Articles 15–17 contain special provisions for jurisdiction over consumer contracts in order to protect the perceived economically weaker and legally less experienced party of the consumer.

Article 15 operates as a definitional provision and provides clarity as to the meaning of "consumer" and "consumer contract". Under Art 15(1) a person will be considered to be a consumer if he concluded a contract for a purpose which can be regarded as being outside his trade or profession. If a person concludes a contract for the purchase of goods to be used for mixed purposes which are in part within and in part outside his trade or profession then these special provisions shall not apply unless it can be shown that the trade or professional purpose is so limited as to be negligible in the overall context of the supply (*Gruber* v *Bay Wa AG* (2006)).

Articles 15(1)(a), (b) and (c), in conjunction with Art 15(3), provide clarification with regard to what is, and is not, considered to be a consumer contract. Article 15(1)(c) extends these protective provisions to contracts concluded by the consumer with a person who pursues commercial or professional activities in the Member State of the consumer's domicile or, by any means, directs such activities to that Member State, or to several states including that Member State, and the contract falls within the scope of such activities. The meaning of "directing activities" in the context of electronic consumer transactions was considered by the European Court in the joined cases of *Pammer* v *Reederei Karl Schluter GmbH & Co KG* and *Hotel Alpenhof GmbH* v *Heller* (2011). The Court held that the mere accessibility of a trader's website in the Member State in which the consumer is domiciled does not constitute the directing of activities. Instead, it had to be ascertained whether, before the conclusion of any contract with the consumer, it was apparent from the trader's websites and overall activity that the trader envisaged doing business with consumers domiciled in the Member State of the consumer's domicile in the sense that the trader was minded to conclude a contract with those consumers.

Once a party is considered to be a consumer who has concluded a consumer contract within the terms of Art 15 then Art 16 provides similar protection to that available in matters relating to insurance. Thus, the consumer may bring proceedings in his "home" court against a party domiciled in a different Member State (Art 16(1)), including a party with a deemed domicile (Art 15(2)), while proceedings may be brought against the consumer in the courts of his domicile only (Art 16(2)), subject to the exceptions found in Arts 15(1) and 16(3). Article 17 limits the enforceability of "choice of court" agreements in order to protect consumers by preventing businesses from inserting jurisdiction clauses that waive or alter these protective rules. Once again, these rules of protective jurisdiction are subject to Art 24, which in the future will include the protective notification requirement under Art 26 of the recast Regulation when the consumer is the defendant.

Individual contracts of employment

Section 5 of the Brussels I Regulation provides an almost comprehensive set of jurisdictional rules, subject to the exceptions found in Arts 18(1) and 20(2), for individual contracts of employment. Under Art 19 an employer domiciled in a Member State, including an employer with a deemed domicile (Art 18(2)), may be sued not only in that state but also in another Member State in the courts for the place where the employee habitually carries out his work or in the courts for the last place where he did so or, if the employee does not or did not habitually carry out his work in any one country, in the courts for the place where the business which engaged the employee is or was situated. In contrast, the employee may be sued only in the courts of the Member State in which he is domiciled (Art 20(1)).

As with the other grounds of protective jurisdiction, the enforceability of "choice of court" agreements is limited to circumstances in which such an agreement will not be detrimental to the weaker party, in this case the employee (Art 21). Article 24 is applicable to individual contracts of employment in the same manner as for matters relating to insurance and consumer contracts, including the caveat to be added under the new Art 26 of the recast Regulation when the employee is the defendant. The recast Regulation extends the scope of the protective jurisdiction provisions to actions against employers domiciled outside the European Union and also permits recourse to the co-defendant provisions of the current Art 6(1) (new Art 8(1)) but only in the case of proceedings brought against an employer.

Exclusive jurisdiction

Article 22 of the Brussels I Regulation identifies a number of circumstances in which the courts of a particular Member State will be considered to have exclusive jurisdiction. Article 22 is mandatory and will prevent recourse to any other jurisdictional ground. In particular, the functioning of Art 22 remains unaffected by any agreements as to jurisdiction or by the submission of the defendant to a jurisdiction other than that identified under Art 22. Article 22 applies regardless of domicile, with the consequence that it applies even if neither party is domiciled in an EU state. Broadly speaking, exclusive jurisdiction is allocated in relation to certain proceedings concerned with immovable property, corporations, public registers, intellectual property and the enforcement of judgments.

"Choice of court" clauses

Under Art 23(1) of the Brussels I Regulation if parties, one or more of whom is domiciled in a Member State, have agreed that a court or the courts of a Member State are to have jurisdiction to settle any disputes which have arisen or which may arise in connection with a particular legal relationship, that court or those courts shall have jurisdiction. The Regulation therefore respects party autonomy by permitting the prorogation of jurisdiction in that parties may yield to the jurisdiction of a court to which they would not otherwise be subject. Parties are free to identify any Member State of their choosing, there is no requirement for any pre-existing connection to the chosen forum. Further, it is possible for a "choice of court" clause to be effective even if it does not directly state the identity of the Member State in which proceedings should be brought, as long as the Member State chosen can be identified (*Coreck Maritime GmbH v Handelsveem BV* (2000)).

Article 23(1) contains a rebuttable presumption that any court identified in such a clause will have exclusive jurisdiction over the dispute. As this is a rebuttable presumption, parties remain free to agree a non-exclusive jurisdiction clause. If the clause is exclusive then it will operate as to exclude any otherwise applicable ground of jurisdiction under the Regulation apart from those exclusive grounds of jurisdiction under Art 22 (Art 23(5)). As discussed above, the effectiveness of a "choice of court" agreement may also be limited in the context of matters relating to insurance, consumer contracts and individual contracts of employment. An exclusive choice of jurisdiction under Art 23 may also be superseded by Art 24.

Formal requirements

Before a "choice of court" agreement will be effective it must satisfy certain requirements of formal validity which are detailed in Art 23(1). These are that the agreement must be in writing or evidenced in writing; or in a form which accords with practices which the parties have established between themselves; or, in international trade or commerce, in a form which accords with a usage of which the parties are or ought to have been aware and which in such trade or commerce is widely known to, and regularly observed by, parties to contracts of the type involved in the particular trade or commerce concerned. These requirements are absolute and may not be augmented or abated by the provisions of national laws of Member States (*Elefanten Schuh GmbH* v *Jacqmain* (1981)). Any communication by electronic means which provides a durable record of the agreement shall be equivalent to "writing" (Art 23(2)). Matters of substantive validity (principally consent) are not currently addressed by the Regulation but under the recast Regulation such matters will be referred to the law of the courts of the Member State identified in the "choice of court" clause.

Parties not domiciled in a Member State

Article 23(1) applies only when at least one of the parties is domiciled in a Member State. Jurisdiction clauses in favour of the courts of a Member State which are entered into by parties neither of whom are domiciled in a Member State are governed by Art 23(3). Under this provision a choice of a court or the courts of a Member State by such parties will be effective to prevent the courts of other Member States taking jurisdiction. However, there is an important difference between Art 23(1) and Art 23(3) in that, under the former, the court identified in such a clause *must* accept jurisdiction, whereas, under the terms of the latter, a court identified thereunder may decline jurisdiction should it so wish. This distinction will disappear under the recast Regulation with the scope of what is currently Art 23(1) being expanded to apply to all parties, regardless of domicile.

2005 Hague Convention on Choice of Court Agreements

Article 23 applies only when a "choice of court" agreement identifies a court or the courts of a Member State, and this restriction remains in the recast Regulation. Consequently, if a "choice of court" agreement is made in favour of a court or the courts of a jurisdiction outside the European Union then Art 23 will not apply. Such an agreement (and certain others) may in the future be regulated by the terms of the Hague Convention of 30 June 2005 on Choice of Court Agreements. This Convention has been acceded to by Mexico and signed by the United States and the European

Union but is yet to come into force. After coming into force, the Hague Convention will apply in all cases where one or more parties reside in a Contracting State other than an EU Member State.

Submission

Article 24 states that, apart from jurisdiction derived from other provisions of the Regulation, a court of a Member State before which a defendant enters an appearance shall have jurisdiction. Accordingly, if a defendant submits to the jurisdiction of the court then that court will be permitted to hear the dispute even if it would not otherwise have jurisdiction under the Regulation. There are two limits on this jurisdictional basis. First, it does not apply when the defendant enters an appearance to challenge or contest the jurisdiction of the court, even if at the same time he makes submissions in his defence on the substance. Second, the principle of submission does not apply where another court has exclusive jurisdiction by virtue of Art 22. In contrast, Art 24 can be relied upon even if a valid "choice of court" agreement exists under Art 23. In these circumstances submission under the former overrides an earlier agreement under the latter. As identified above, the recast Regulation will introduce a protective requirement of notification in matters relating to insurance, consumer contracts and individual contracts of employment when the submitting party is the perceived weaker party.

Conflicts of jurisdiction

It is possible under the Brussels I Regulation that the courts in two or more Member States will be allocated jurisdiction. For example, the courts of one state may have jurisdiction under the Art 2 ground of the defendant's domicile while the courts in another state may be able to take jurisdiction under one of the Art 5 grounds of special jurisdiction. Indeed, a multiplicity of jurisdictions may even be possible within the same article. If a choice of jurisdiction is apparent then the claimant may choose the Member State in which to initiate his action but the risk remains that proceedings in relation to what is essentially the same dispute and between the same parties may be commenced in two or more jurisdictions. If these proceedings are allowed to complete this could potentially lead to different courts giving conflicting and irreconcilable judgments, not to mention the increased litigation costs of the parties.

Article 27 of the Regulation attempts to limit potential conflicts of jurisdiction by adopting the *lis pendens* system of jurisdiction allocation which places a significant emphasis on the priority of process. This article states that where proceedings involving the same cause of action and between the same parties are brought in the courts of different Member States, any court other than the court first seised shall of its own motion stay its proceedings until such time as the jurisdiction of the court first seised is established. If the jurisdiction of the court first seised is established then any court other than the court first seised must decline jurisdiction in favour of that court. Article 30 provides clarity as regards when a court shall be deemed to be seised. This article applies regardless of the domicile of the parties.

The "first come, first served" rule of Art 27 is one of strict priority and it is important to note its mandatory nature in that the court first seised, once its jurisdiction is established, must accept jurisdiction. Similarly, a court seised later must stay it proceedings until the court first seised has determined whether or not it has jurisdiction. The European Court has held that Art 27 will apply even if there is an exclusive "choice of court" agreement in favour of a court seised later (*Erich Gasser GmbH* v *MISAT Srl* (2005)). The court identified in such a clause will consequently be required to stay its own proceedings until the court first seised has declared that is has no jurisdiction. This decision has been criticised for encouraging a party to adopt delaying tactics by commencing proceedings, often of a negative nature, before a court other than that identified in a jurisdiction clause, in order to delay the determination of the dispute in the previously chosen forum. This problem is exacerbated by the subsequent decision of the European Court in *Turner* v *Grovit* (2005) in which the court held that the use of anti-suit injunctions to prevent vexatious litigation constituted an interference with the jurisdiction of a foreign court and was therefore incompatible with the Regulation.

These criticisms have been addressed in the recast Regulation with the new instrument reversing the decision in *Erich Gasser GmbH* v *MISAT Srl* by giving priority to the court specified in a jurisdiction clause, regardless of whether or not it is the court first seised. Accordingly, the new Art 31(2) states that where an agreement confers exclusive jurisdiction on the court of a Member State then, once this court is seised, any court of another Member State shall stay its proceedings until such time as the chosen court declares that it has no jurisdiction. The recast Regulation thus reverses the priority of process so that, in the future, a "choice of court" agreement will take precedence over the "first in time" rule.

Article 28 applies to actions that are considered to be related to one another even if they do not involve the same cause of action and may be between different parties. In these circumstances any court other than the court first seised may stay its proceedings and possibly decline jurisdiction if the court first seised has jurisdiction over the actions in question and its law permits the consolidation thereof. Actions are deemed to be related where they are so closely connected that it is expedient to hear and determine them together to avoid the risk of irreconcilable judgments resulting from separate proceedings. In contrast to Art 27, under Art 28 a notable amount of discretion is conferred on the later court to decide whether the actions are related and, if so, whether proceedings should be stayed.

Forum non conveniens

In contrast to the strict system of *lis pendens* enforced in the Brussels I Regulation, under the common law of Scotland the doctrine of *forum non conveniens* permits a defender to request that a court should decline to exercise jurisdiction because there is some other tribunal, having competent jurisdiction, in which the case may be tried more suitably for the interests of all the parties and for the ends of justice (*Sim* v *Robinow* (1892)). A plea of *forum non conveniens* may be made whether or not proceedings have already been initiated abroad. The burden of proof is on the defender to show that there is a competent and more appropriate forum available elsewhere. The appropriateness of the alternative forum will be considered in order to determine whether it is the natural forum with the most real and substantial connection to the dispute in terms of the convenience of the parties, the availability of witnesses, the applicable law, whether proceedings have already been initiated in the identified court, or if related proceedings are under way in either court. The existence of an exclusive jurisdiction clause in favour of a particular court is considered to be a very strong factor in this determination. If the existence of a clearly more appropriate forum is established then a plea of *forum non conveniens* will be accepted unless the pursuer can show that requiring him to litigate in this forum would be unjust. The pursuer could thus argue that he would be denied justice in the clearly more appropriate forum because of issues such as the cost of litigation, procedural delays, or concerns over the competence or fairness of the identified courts. The mere fact that this alternative forum may not be as advantageous to the pursuer is not enough to constitute a denial of justice.

Reliance on the doctrine of *forum non conveniens* will be competent only where to do so is not inconsistent with what is now the Brussels I Regulation or the Lugano Convention (CJJA 1982, s 49). A plea of *forum non conveniens* can therefore be made in cases falling within Sch 4 to the 1982 Act (intra-UK cases) and s 22(1) of the 1982 Act states that nothing in Sch 8 (the residual Scottish rules) shall prevent the court from declining jurisdiction on the ground of *forum non conveniens*. However, the European Court has held that a court of a Member State is precluded from declining the jurisdiction conferred on it by Art 2 on the ground that a court of a

non-Member State would be a more appropriate forum, even if the jurisdiction of no other Member State is in issue and the proceedings have no
connection to any other Member State (*Owusu* v *Jackson* (2005)).

Under the recast Regulation the effects of the decision in *Owusu* will
be ameliorated partially by the introduction of elements of the doctrine
of *forum non conveniens* into the Brussels regime when an action is pending
before the court of a (non-EU) third state at the time when a court in a
Member State is seised of an action which is related to the action in the
court of the third state. The new Art 34 thus gives a Member State court
a limited discretion to stay its proceedings when proceedings have been
initiated first in a third state but only when the requirements of that article
are met in that it is expedient to hear and determine the related actions
together to avoid the risk of irreconcilable judgments resulting from separate proceedings; it is expected that the court of the third state will give
a judgment capable of recognition and, where applicable, of enforcement
in that Member State; and the court of the Member State is satisfied that
a stay is necessary for the proper administration of justice. Recital (24)
provides guidance concerning the circumstances relevant to the proper
administration of justice.

INTRA-UNITED KINGDOM CASES

Section 16 of the CJJA 1982 applies a modified form of the jurisdictional
provisions of the Brussels I Regulation as between the different parts of the
United Kingdom. These modified rules are set out in Sch 4 (as amended by
the Civil Jurisdiction and Judgments Order 2001, Sch 2) and apply when
the subject-matter of the proceedings is within the scope of the Regulation
and the defendant is domiciled in the United Kingdom or the proceedings
are of a kind mentioned in Art 22 of the Regulation (exclusive jurisdiction regardless of domicile). Schedule 4 has two main functions in that it
will provide identification of a specific territorial unit when the Brussels I
Regulation allocates jurisdiction to the United Kingdom generally and it
also applies in cases which are internal to the United Kingdom but are
related to more than one territorial unit thereof. Although Sch 4 appears
very similar to the terms of the Regulation, there are four key differences
between the provisions of Sch 4 and the corresponding provisions of the
Regulation, as discussed earlier in this chapter:

(1) The rules of special jurisdiction in matters relating to contract
     refer to the courts for the place of performance of the obligation
     in question and do not include the bespoke provisions under the

Regulation relating to contracts for the sale of goods or the provision of services (Sch 4, r 3(a)).

(2) The articles in the Regulation regulating jurisdiction in matters relating to insurance are not replicated in Sch 4.

(3) In relation to "choice of court" agreements, Sch 4, unlike Art 23 of the Regulation, contains no presumption of exclusivity, nor requirements as to writing (Sch 4, r 12).

(4) As identified above, the provisions in the Regulation relating to *lis pendens* are excluded from Sch 4.

Essential Facts

- There are four regimes governing the jurisdiction of the Scottish courts: the Brussels I Regulation; the 2007 Lugano Convention; the Civil Jurisdiction and Judgments Act 1982, Sch 4; and the Civil Jurisdiction and Judgments Act 1982, Sch 8.
- Article 2 of the Brussels I Regulation provides that the general ground of jurisdiction is the domicile of the defendant. Domicile is given a specific definition for both individuals (CJJA 1982, s 41 as amended by the Civil Jurisdiction and Judgments Order 2001, Sch 1, para 9) and companies (Art 60).
- Article 5 provides alternative grounds of special jurisdiction when there is a close link between the subject-matter of the dispute and the forum – most notably in matters relating to contract and delict.
- Grounds of protective jurisdiction apply in matters relating to insurance (Arts 8–14), consumer contracts (Arts 15–17) and individual contracts of employment (Arts 18–21).
- Article 22 identifies a number of circumstances in which the courts of a particular Member State will be considered to have exclusive jurisdiction.
- Article 23 permits the prorogation of jurisdiction of a court or courts of a Member State by parties. They is no requirement for any pre-existing connection to the chosen forum.
- Article 24 will clothe the court of a Member State with jurisdiction should the defendant enter an appearance, provided that such appearance was not solely or primarily made in order to challenge or contest that jurisdiction.
- The Regulation attempts to limit potential conflicts of jurisdiction by adopting a "first come, first served" rule under Art 27.

• In cases falling outside the ambit of the Brussels I Regulation and the Lugano Convention, the Scottish courts may utilise the doctrine of *forum non conveniens* in order to identify a more appropriate forum.

Essential Cases

De Bloos SPRL v Bouyer SA (1976): the "place of performance of the obligation in question" in Art 5(1)(a) refers to the obligation which forms the basis of the legal proceedings.

Handelswekerij GJ Bier BV v Mines de Potasse d'Alsace SA (1978): the "place where the harmful event occurred or may occur" in Art 5(3) refers to both the place where the damage occurred and the place of the event which gives rise to this damage.

Shevill v Presse Alliance SA (1995): in a claim of damage to reputation in the context of a multi-state defamation the claimant has the option under Art 5(3) of bringing his action in either the courts of the place of publication or in the courts of any place in which the publication was distributed and where damage to reputation is sustained.

Dumez France SA v Hessische Landesbank (1990): Art 5(3) is limited to the place where the harmful event actually occurs, not the place where the claimant feels the adverse consequences of this event.

Pammer v Reederei Karl Schluter GmbH & Co KG (2011): the mere accessibility of a trader's website in a Member State does not, by itself, constitute a directing of activities for the purposes of Art 15.

Erich Gasser GmbH v MISAT Srl (2005): Art 27 (priority of process) will apply even if the court seised first was seised in violation of an exclusive "choice of court" agreement.

Owusu v Jackson (2005): if a court assumes jurisdiction under the Regulation then it is precluded from utilising the doctrine of *forum non conveniens*.

4 RECOGNITION AND ENFORCEMENT OF FOREIGN DECREES

The precise rules for the recognition and enforcement in the United Kingdom of judgments emanating from the courts of another country are determined by the geographical location of what is referred to as the court of origin. If that court is situated in the territory of an EU or EFTA Member State then the recognition and enforcement provisions of the Brussels I Regulation or the 2007 Lugano Convention are applicable respectively. If the court of origin is situated in a jurisdiction to which the Administration of Justice Act 1920 or the Foreign Judgments (Reciprocal Enforcement) Act 1933 applies then judgments therefrom will be subject to the enforcement procedure contained in the relevant Act. The recognition and enforcement of the judgments of a court of origin which is situated in a jurisdiction that is neither an EU/EFTA Member State, nor subject to the terms of the 1920 Act or 1933 Act, will be determined under the common law. Provision also exists under the Civil Jurisdiction and Judgments Act 1982 for the recognition and enforcement of a judgment granted in one part of the United Kingdom in the other parts thereof. This chapter will consider each of these regimes.

THE RECOGNITION AND ENFORCEMENT OF FOREIGN JUDGMENTS AT COMMON LAW

Enforcement via the common law will be necessary when a judgment originates from a foreign country which is not bound by the Brussels I Regulation/the 2007 Lugano Convention, nor linked by reciprocal arrangements with the United Kingdom under the Administration of Justice Act 1920 or the Foreign Judgments (Reciprocal Enforcement) Act 1933. Before a foreign decree *in personam* will be enforced in Scotland the foreign court of origin must have had jurisdiction to grant the decree. Once jurisdiction is established then the judgment will be recognised unless one of the limited number of defences to recognition can be established.

Jurisdiction

It is fundamental to the recognition and enforcement in Scotland of a foreign judgment that the court of origin is regarded by Scots law as having had jurisdiction over the action to which the judgment relates. This question will be determined not with reference to the domestic understanding of jurisdiction (whether of the court of origin or the Scottish courts) but according to the classification of jurisdiction in an international context. By this standard, certain grounds of jurisdiction will be considered acceptable while others will be considered exorbitant and thus unacceptable. The former category includes jurisdiction on the basis of the residence or presence of the defender, with temporary physical presence considered sufficient (*Adams* v *Cape Industries Plc* (1990)). Jurisdiction will be granted over a corporate defender if the corporation carries on business within the territory of the court, although the mere fact that a company has a website accessible in a particular country does not automatically mean that it is carrying on business there (*Lucasfilm Ltd* v *Ainsworth* (2009)). Jurisdiction will also be accepted if taken on grounds of prorogation, submission or reconvention (counterclaims). In contrast, jurisdiction exercised on the basis of domicile (in its traditional form), nationality, the ownership of immoveable property (in actions unrelated to that property) or the arrestment of moveables would not be recognised under the common law of Scotland.

Defences

Even if a foreign court has taken jurisdiction on an acceptable basis, the subsequent decree may still be refused recognition under the common law on some other ground. First, a foreign decree resulting from a penal or revenue action will not be enforced in Scotland. The Protection of Trading Interests Act 1980 also prohibits the enforcement under the common law of those judgments identified within that Act. Second, a foreign judgment may also be challenged on the ground of fraud. Such challenge may allege that the fraudulent behaviour was attributable to the court, the other party to the proceedings, or both. Third, enforcement could be resisted where the decree is contrary to natural justice because of some form of procedural irregularity, although a mere difference to the procedural rules applicable in Scotland will not be sufficient. Fourthly, a foreign judgment could be challenged on the ground of public policy.

A foreign decree will be enforced in Scotland only if it is considered to be "final". A decree which is interlocutory and liable to variation or alteration will not be enforced. However, a foreign decree need not be final in the sense that it cannot be made the subject of appeal to a higher court in the country of origin but it must be final and unalterable in the court which pronounced it (*Nouvion* v *Freeman* (1889)). It is important to note that it is not a relevant objection to a foreign judgment that the court came to a mistaken conclusion, either on the facts or on the law. The merits of a foreign decree will not normally be examined, except in cases where fraud is alleged. If a party believes that a foreign case was decided incorrectly then this should be challenged under the foreign legal system, not as a means by which to resist enforcement in Scotland.

Enforcement

At common law, a foreign decree is enforced in Scotland by raising an action for decree conform in the Court of Session. Decree conform may be granted only against a person who was a party to the foreign proceedings and who is personally liable under that judgment by the law of the foreign court. An action for decree conform is incompetent when the judgment which it is sought to enforce may be enforced under the provisions of the Foreign Judgments (Reciprocal Enforcement) Act 1933, the Brussels I Regulation, the 2007 Lugano Convention, or the intra-UK scheme under the Civil Jurisdiction and Judgments Act 1982. A decree conform may be sought even if the foreign judgment comes within the terms of the Administration of Justice Act 1920, but the pursuer may not be able to recover the expenses of the action (s 9(5)). A foreign decree may also be founded upon for purposes of *res judicata* as a defence to an action on the same ground in Scotland.

STATUTORY SCHEMES FOR THE RECOGNITION AND ENFORCEMENT OF FOREIGN JUDGMENTS

Apart from the common-law method of obtaining a decree conform, a foreign judgment may be enforced in Scotland by compliance with those statutory procedures which facilitate the registration and subsequent enforcement of a foreign judgment as though it were a Scottish judgment. The two most important statutes are the Administration of Justice Act 1920 and the Foreign Judgments (Reciprocal Enforcement) Act 1933. The former applies only to Commonwealth countries whereas the latter applies also to judgments of courts in politically foreign countries. Both Acts are dependent upon reciprocity.

Administration of Justice Act 1920

Part II of the Administration of Justice Act 1920 provides for the enforcement within Scotland, and other parts of the United Kingdom, of certain judgments of the superior courts of Commonwealth countries which make reciprocal provisions for the enforcement of the judgments emanating from the corresponding courts of the United Kingdom. The Act applies only to countries specified by Orders in Council and, while no new countries may now be specified, the extant provisions remain in force (ss 13 and 14). The

1920 Act applies only to judgments or orders made by a superior court in civil proceedings whereby a sum of money is made payable (s 12(1)). Such a judgment may be enforced in Scotland on application to the Court of Session, with the Scottish court retaining a discretion to register and enforce the foreign judgment only if it thinks it just and convenient to do so (s 9(1)).

A foreign judgment may not be registered if the original court acted without jurisdiction (s 9(2)(a)); the defender, being a person who was neither carrying on business nor ordinarily resident within the jurisdiction of the original court, did not voluntarily appear or otherwise submit or agree to submit to the jurisdiction of that court (s 9(2)(b)); or the defender was not duly served with the process of the original court and did not appear, notwithstanding that he was ordinarily resident or was carrying on business within the jurisdiction of that court or agreed to submit to the jurisdiction of that court (s 9(2)(c)). An external judgment that otherwise comes within the terms of the 1920 Act may also be refused recognition and enforcement if it was obtained by fraud (s 9(2)(d)); if an appeal is pending, or the defender is entitled and intends to appeal (s 9(2)(e)); or if it is contrary to public policy (s 9(2)(f)).

When the foreign judgment is registered it will then be enforced as a decree of the Court of Session, with the same force and effect as if it had been a judgment originally obtained in that court (s 9(3)(a)). The court shall have the same control and jurisdiction over the judgment as it has over similar judgments given by itself, but only in so far as relates to execution (s 9(3)(b)).

Foreign Judgments (Reciprocal Enforcement) Act 1933

The 1933 Act provides further provision for the enforcement within the United Kingdom of the judgments of the courts of foreign countries, including, but not limited to, those of the Commonwealth. Whereas the 1920 Act applies only to the judgments of superior courts, the 1933 Act makes reciprocal enforcement of the judgments of any recognised court within a foreign country, with both the country and the recognised court, or courts, specified by Orders in Council. Such an Order will be made only after the Crown is satisfied that substantial reciprocity of treatment will be assured as regards the enforcement in that country of similar judgments given in similar courts of the United Kingdom (s 1). The 1933 Act remains applicable to states party to the Brussels I Regulation and the 2007 Lugano Convention in relation to matters to which the Regulation and Convention do not apply.

Following registration under the 1933 Act, a foreign judgment will be enforced in Scotland as if it were a Court of Session decree. Before registration will be permitted the judgment must be either final and conclusive or require the judgment debtor to make an interim payment to the judgment creditor. A judgment is considered final and conclusive notwithstanding that it may be subject to appeal or that an appeal is pending against it (s 1(3)). In addition, the judgment must require the payment of a sum of money, not being a sum payable in respect of taxes or other charges of a like nature, or in respect of a fine or other penalty (s 1(2)). A judgment from a recognised court will not be enforced where it is given on appeal from a court which is not a recognised court or if its purpose was for the enforcement of a judgment given in a third country (s 1(2A)).

Section 4(1)(a) contains grounds upon which a registration shall be set aside, including: where the court of origin had no jurisdiction; the defender did not receive notice of those proceedings in sufficient time to enable him to defend the proceedings and did not appear; the judgment was obtained by fraud; or the enforcement of the judgment would be contrary to public policy in the country of the registering court. As regards jurisdiction, s 4(2) and s 4(3) detail when a foreign court will, and will not, be deemed to have had jurisdiction. A foreign judgment to which the 1933 Act applies may not be enforced except by way of registration under the Act (s 6). Unlike the position under the 1920 Act, where registration is discretionary, registration under the 1933 Act is a matter of right, provided that the judgment has not been wholly satisfied or it could not be enforced by execution in the country of the original court (s 2(1)).

RECOGNITION AND ENFORCEMENT OF JUDGMENTS UNDER THE BRUSSELS I REGULATION AND THE 2007 LUGANO CONVENTION

The jurisdictional provisions of the Brussels I Regulation were discussed in Chapter 3. The requirement of all Member States to adopt uniform grounds of jurisdiction under the Regulation is reflected in the permissiveness of the rules of recognition and enforcement contained in Arts 32–56 which are designed to ensure that a judgment given in one Member State will move freely throughout the European Union. The principle on which the Regulation is based is the desire to minimise the obstacles to the recognition and enforcement of judgments issued from the courts of Member States, notably by restricting the ability of the court of a Member State in which enforcement is sought to review the jurisdiction of the court of origin. The same principle underpins the 2007 Lugano Convention, the text of which is aligned with that of the Brussels I Regulation, meaning that what is said below regarding the latter instrument applies *mutatis mutandis* to the former.

The recognition and enforcement rules of the Regulation apply only to judgments of Member States within the scope of the Regulation as defined in Art 1. The Regulation applies to any species of judgment, not only money judgments, including interim orders as well as final orders. Unlike the position under the Acts of 1920 and 1933, there is no restriction of the provisions to the judgments of certain courts and Art 1(1) states that the Regulation applies whatever the nature of the court or tribunal. The enforcement procedure under the Regulation applies to all judgments within its scope, whether or not they are against persons domiciled in a Member State and whether or not the court of origin assumed jurisdiction on a ground set out in the Regulation or on a residual ground of jurisdiction found in its national law. In light of this, Art 59 of the 1968 Brussels Convention permitted Contracting States to enter a binding agreement with a non-Contracting State to the effect that it would not recognise judgments given in other Contracting States against defendants domiciled or habitually resident in that non-Contracting State when the court of origin based its jurisdiction on a residual ground. The effect of such agreements is preserved under the Regulation, but no new agreements may be made (Art 72).

Recognition

Article 33(1) of the Regulation provides that a judgment given in a Member State shall be recognised in the other Member States without any special procedure being required. Articles 34 and 35 provide limited grounds for the refusal of recognition. Article 34(1) provides that a judgment shall not be recognised if such recognition is manifestly contrary to public policy in the Member State in which recognition is sought. Recourse to public policy will be permitted only in exceptional circumstances where recognition would be at variance to an unacceptable degree with the legal order of the Member State in which enforcement is sought in as much as it infringes a fundamental principle of that state (*Bamberski* v *Krombach* (2001)). The world "manifestly" did not appear in the 1968 Brussels Convention but was included in the Regulation to emphasise the exceptional nature of the circumstances justifying refusal under this ground. The court in which recognition is sought may not review the merits of the judgment (Art 36), nor apply the test of public policy to the grounds of jurisdiction relied on by the court of origin (Art 35(3)).

Article 34(2) provides that a judgment shall not be recognised where it was given in default of appearance, if the defendant was not served with the document which instituted the proceedings or with an equivalent document in sufficient time and in such a way as to enable him to arrange for his defence, unless the defendant failed to commence proceedings to challenge the judgment when it was possible for him to do so. Article 34(3) and (4) permit non-recognition of a judgment when it is irreconcilable with a judgment given in a dispute between the same parties in the Member State in which recognition is sought or when it is irreconcilable with an earlier judgment given in another Member State or in a third State involving the same cause of action and between the same parties, provided that the earlier judgment fulfils the conditions necessary for its recognition in the Member State addressed.

Article 35(1) requires Member States to refuse to recognise a judgment which conflicts with the mandatory provisions applicable in matters relating to insurance consumer contracts, or the grounds of exclusive jurisdiction discussed in the previous chapter. However, even in these circumstances, the court in which recognition is sought will still be bound by the findings of fact on which the court of origin based its jurisdiction.

Enforcement

A judgment given in a Member State and enforceable in that state shall be enforced in Scotland when, on the application of any interested party, it has been registered for enforcement (Art 38). This terminology differs slightly from the general requirement applicable to all other Member States that a judgment will be enforceable once it has been "declared enforceable" (known as the *exequatur* procedure). There is no equivalent of a declaration of enforceability in the United Kingdom, so reference is made instead to the judgment being "registered for enforcement".

Registration of the judgment is a prerequisite to enforcement but the procedure of registration is essentially of an administrative nature, with the party against whom enforcement is sought not being entitled to be heard at this stage of the proceedings (Art 41). This party does not even have the right to be informed of the application for registration, with such absence of notice being deliberate in order to preserve the element of surprise and prevent the removal of assets from the Member State in which enforcement is sought. Once registered, the judgment will have the same force and effect as if it had originally been given by the registering court, with enforcement powers and proceedings available on that basis. Articles 43–46 detail the circumstances in which an appeal can be made against a declaration of enforceability, with Art 45 providing that a court considering an appeal may set aside registration only on one of the grounds specified in Arts 34 and 35 (discussed above in the context of recognition).

One of the key changes to be introduced under the recast Regulation is the abolition of *exequatur* as a necessary prior step to enforcement. Accordingly, under the recast Regulation a judgment given in one Member State will be recognised in all other Member States without any specific procedure and, if enforceable in the Member State of origin, will be enforceable in the other Member States without any declaration of enforceability (registration for enforcement in the United Kingdom) being required. This move follows similar developments in other areas in which the European Union has passed specialist measures to facilitate enforcement without *exequatur* in relation to uncontested claims (Regulation 805/2004); a special European order for payment procedure (Regulation 1896/2006); and a European small claims procedure (Regulation 861/2007).

RECIPROCAL ENFORCEMENT WITHIN THE UNITED KINGDOM

Sections 18 and 19 of and Schs 6 and 7 to the Civil Jurisdiction and Judgments Act 1982 provide for the enforcement in one part of the United Kingdom of a judgment emanating from another part thereof where that judgment falls within the ambit of ss 18 and 19. Schedule 6 applies to money provisions while Sch 7 applies to non-money provisions. Enforcement is by means of registration, in the court in which enforcement is sought, of a certificate granted by the court of origin. Registration is in the Court of Session only, even if the court of origin was an inferior court. Registration under either Schedule shall be set aside if the registration was contrary to the provisions of the applicable Schedule, and may be set aside if the registering court is satisfied that the matter in dispute had previously been the subject of a judgment by another court having jurisdiction in the matter (Sch 6, para 10; Sch 7, para 9).

Essential Facts

- The rules applicable to the recognition and enforcement of foreign decrees are determined by the geographical location of the court of origin.
- Enforcement via the common law will occur only if the foreign court is considered to have had jurisdiction over the action to which the judgment relates. Jurisdiction is determined on an international, rather than a domestic, basis.
- A statutory scheme for the reciprocal recognition and enforcement of foreign judgments exists under the Administration of Justice Act 1920 and the Foreign Judgments (Reciprocal Enforcement) Act 1933.

- The Brussels I Regulation provides permissive rules of recognition and enforcement in order to facilitate the free movement of judgments between Member States. Equivalent provisions are included in the 2007 Lugano Convention.
- The reciprocal enforcement of judgments between the different parts of the United Kingdom is governed by the Civil Jurisdiction and Judgments Act 1982, ss 18 and 19 and Schs 6 and 7.

Essential Cases

Adams v Cape Industries Plc (1990): temporary physical presence is considered an acceptable basis of jurisdiction under the common law.

Nouvion v Freeman (1889): before a foreign judgment will be recognised and enforced under the common law it must be final and unalterable in the court of origin.

Bamberski v Krombach (2001): recourse to the public policy exception of the Brussels I Regulation is permitted only when recognition would be at variance to an unacceptable degree with the legal order of the Member State in which enforcement is sought in as much as it infringes a fundamental principle of that state.

5 CHOICE OF LAW IN CONTRACT

The rules applicable to choice of law in contract are now found in Regulation (EC) No 593/2008 of the European Parliament and of the Council of 17 June 2008 on the law applicable to contractual obligations, commonly referred to as the "Rome I Regulation". This Regulation completely replaces the earlier Rome Convention on the Law Applicable to Contractual Obligations 1980, commonly referred to as the "1980 Rome Convention" and brought into force in the United Kingdom by the Contracts (Applicable Law) Act 1990. The 1980 Rome Convention came into effect in the United Kingdom on 1 April 1991 and applied to contracts concluded between that date and 16 December 2009. The Rome I Regulation applies to contracts concluded as from 17 December 2009. Thus, although replaced as from 17 December 2009, the 1980 Rome Convention will continue to be relevant for the foreseeable future, as its provisions remain applicable to disputes relating to contracts concluded before that date. This chapter will primarily consider the provisions of the Regulation but reference will be made to the terms of the Convention as and when appropriate. The common law remains applicable to contracts concluded before 1 April 1991 and to contracts concluded after that date but which fall outside the scope of the Convention or the Regulation. The limited relevance of these common-law rules means that they will not be considered in this chapter.

SCOPE

The scope of the Rome I Regulation is stated positively in Art 1(1) in that it shall apply, in situations involving a conflict of laws, to contractual obligations in civil and commercial matters. Although the equivalent article of the 1980 Rome Convention uses a slightly different formulation, there would appear to be no material difference in the two provisions. In order to ensure consistency, the term "civil and commercial matters" is to be interpreted in the same way as under the Brussels I Regulation. The term "contractual obligations" is left undefined and the question as to whether or not an obligation is considered to be a contractual one will be regarded as a matter to be decided by the European Court as a matter of EU law. Article 1(1) also limits the scope of the Regulation by stating that it shall not apply to revenue, customs or administrative matters. Again, this phrase is to be interpreted consistently with the identical wording found in the Brussels I Regulation. The scope of the Regulation is also narrowed by the express exclusion of certain matters as detailed in Art 1(2) and (3). Article 2 states that the law specified by the Regulation shall be applied whether or not it is the law of a Member State. Under this principle of universal application the Regulation, and the Convention before it, does not discriminate in its selection of the applicable law and the law of a non-EU Member State will be treated identically to the law of an EU Member State.

A composite state, such as the United Kingdom, is not required to apply the Regulation to internal conflicts between the laws of different territorial units within that state (Art 22(2)). However, in the interests of simplicity and uniformity of application, the United Kingdom has opted to extend the rules of the Regulation to intra-UK conflicts (for Scotland, see the Law Applicable to Contractual Obligations (Scotland) Regulations 2009 (SSI 2009/410)).

APPLICABLE LAW BY CHOICE

Recital (11) of the Rome I Regulation states that "The parties' freedom to choose the applicable law should be one of the cornerstones of the system of conflict-of-law rules in matters of contractual obligations". The priority of party autonomy is embodied in Art 3(1) which states that "A contract shall be governed by the law chosen by the parties. The choice shall be made expressly or clearly demonstrated by the terms of the contract or the circumstances of the case". It is important to note that, whether a governing law is chosen by express provision or by implication, parties are completely free to choose this law and there is no requirement that the law have some extant connection to the parties or the contract, ie parties are free to choose a wholly neutral law, otherwise entirely unconnected to their circumstances.

Express choice

Parties can choose expressly the law to govern their contract via the inclusion of a clause in the contract stating that the contract is to be governed by the law of a particular country. Choice of the governing law is limited to the law of a country. In the context of composite states, each territorial unit thereof will be considered as a country for purposes of identifying the applicable law (Art 22(1)). Parties may not choose a religious law, such as Sharia law, to govern their contract (*Beximco Pharmaceuticals Ltd* v *Shamil Bank of Bahrain EC* (2003)).

Implied choice

In many cases a contract may not include an express choice of law but it is nevertheless clear that the parties assumed or intended that the law of a particular country would govern their contract. Such an implied choice will be respected if the choice can be "clearly demonstrated by the terms of the contract or the circumstances of the case". Under the equivalent provision of the Convention it is stated that the choice must be "demonstrated with reasonable certainty". Although not express, a choice of a particular law must be just that – a choice – and a court is not permitted to infer a choice of law that it believes the parties would have chosen, had they applied their minds to the question.

Guidance as to the factors relevant in determining whether the parties have made an implied choice of law is given in the Report on the Convention on the Law Applicable to Contractual Obligations by Professors Mario Giuliano and Paul Lagarde, commonly referred to as the Giuliano–Lagarde Report. This guidance is non-exhaustive but refers to issues such as reliance on a standard form governed by a particular system of law, a previous course of dealing between the parties under contracts that were governed by an express choice of law, an express choice of law made in related transactions between the parties, or the choice of a place where disputes are to be settled by arbitration (p 16). For example, in the case of *Egon Oldendorff* v *Libera Corp (No 2)* (1996) it was held, relying on the terms of the Giuliano–Lagarde Report, that where an international contract between a German company and a Japanese company expressly provided for arbitration in London and was governed by a well-known English standard form of charterparty that, in the absence of an express choice of law, the parties had impliedly chosen English law.

In its identification of those factors relevant in determining an implied choice of law, the Giuliano–Lagarde Report also states that the choice of a particular forum may show in no uncertain manner that the parties intended the contract to be governed by the law of that forum, subject to the other terms of the contract and all the circumstances of the case. During the drafting of the Rome I Regulation it was proposed by the Commission that a presumption should be introduced to the effect that if the parties had chosen the courts of a Member State to govern any disputes arising out of the contract they would be presumed to have chosen the law of that Member State as the governing law. This proposal was not accepted but in Recital (12) to the Regulation it is stated that "An agreement between the parties to confer on one or more courts or tribunals of a Member State exclusive jurisdiction to determine disputes under the contract should be one of the factors to be taken into account in determining whether a choice of law has been clearly demonstrated".

Division of or change in the governing law

The last sentence of Art 3(1) provides that "By their choice the parties can select the law applicable to the whole or to part only of the contract". This allows *dépeçage* – a splitting of the applicable law. This choice is limited by the fact that it must be logically consistent in that each separate choice of law must relate to a part of a contract which is capable of being governed by a different law without giving rise to contradictions. If inconsistency does occur then there is no effective choice by the parties and reference must be made to the terms of Art 4 in order to identify the applicable law. Parties may at any time change the governing law of the contract, either by altering a previously agreed choice or by making a choice where previously they had not done so (Art 3(2)). Any change in the applicable law that is made after the conclusion of the contract shall not prejudice its formal validity or adversely affect the rights of third parties.

Freedom of choice and mandatory rules

The freedom of choice given to parties under Art 3(1) to choose the law applicable to their contract is not absolute and, instead, Art 3(3) operates to prevent parties from evading the mandatory rules of the system of law with which the contract and the parties are otherwise wholly connected. Article 3(3) thus states that "Where all other elements relevant to the situation at the time of the choice are located in a country other than the country whose law has been chosen, the choice of the parties shall not prejudice the application of provisions of the law of that other country which cannot be derogated from by agreement". For example, if all elements relevant to the situation are located in Scotland, the parties will be unable to avoid the mandatory rules of Scots law by agreeing that the law of France is to govern the contract. While this choice will be respected and French law will indeed be the governing law it will be applied subject to the mandatory rules of Scots law. Article 3(3) applies only when all elements relevant to the situation are located in a single country other than the country chosen. If an element can be located elsewhere then Art 3(3) has no application. For the purposes of Art 3(3), the choice of law clause itself and, if present, a "choice of court" clause, are not elements relevant to the situation. In *Emeraldian Ltd Partnership* v *Wellmix Shipping Ltd* (2010), a case decided under Art 3(3) of the 1980 Rome Convention which contains slightly different wording but is ultimately of the same effect, a choice of English law under a contract with very strong connections to China was not subject to the mandatory rules of the latter, as the beneficiary of the contract in issue was a Liberian company.

Similar to Art 3(3), Art 3(4) operates to prevent parties avoiding an otherwise applicable mandatory rule of Union law through choosing the law of a third state by providing that "Where all other elements relevant to the situation at the time of the choice are located in one or more Member States, the parties' choice of applicable law other than that of a Member State shall not prejudice the application of provisions of Community law, where appropriate as implemented in the Member State of the forum, which cannot be derogated from by agreement". It is important to note the wider scope of Art 3(4) in that it applies even when the elements may be located in different countries, as long as those countries are all Member States and the choice is of the law of a third state.

APPLICABLE LAW IN THE ABSENCE OF CHOICE

The Convention

Article 4 of both the Convention and the Regulation determines the law applicable to a contract in the absence of a choice by the parties. Unlike the position with Art 3, there is a significant divergence between Art 4 of the Convention and its counterpart in the Regulation, meaning that the provisions of each instrument must be considered separately. Article 4(1) of the Convention states that "To the extent that the law applicable to the contract has not been chosen in accordance with Article 3, the contract shall be governed by the law of the country with which it is most closely connected". A second sentence provides for the application of *dépeçage*.

Characteristic performance

Article 4(2) attempts to make the identification of the law of the country to which the contract is most closely connected more certain by providing that

> "Subject to the provisions of paragraph 5 of this Article, it shall be presumed that the contract is most closely connected with the country where the party who is to effect the performance which is characteristic of the contract has, at the time of conclusion of the contract, his habitual residence, or, in the case of a body corporate or unincorporate, its central administration. However, if the contract is entered into in the course of that party's trade or profession, that country shall be the country in which the principal place of business is situated or, where under the terms of the contract the performance is to be effected through a place of business other than the principal place of business, the country in which that other place of business is situated".

Article 4(3) provides a special presumption applicable when the subject-matter of the contract is a right in immovable property or a right to use immovable property; while Art 4(4) supplies a special presumption applicable when the contract is for the carriage of goods.

The "performance which is characteristic of the contract" presents little difficulty in the case of unilateral contracts under which the characteristic performance should be clear. In bilateral contracts whereby the parties undertake mutual reciprocal performance, with the counter-performance of one of the parties usually being in the form of a payment of money, it is the performance for which this payment is due, and not the payment itself, which usually constitutes the characteristic performance (for examples of which, see the Giuliano–Lagarde Report, p 20). Thus, in the most common examples of a contract for the sale of goods or the provision of services, the characteristic performance will be the provision of these goods or services. The identification of the characteristic performance will be more difficult, if not impossible, when a complex contract is at issue and recourse may have to be made to Art 4(5), under which the presumption of Art 4(2) will not apply and attention will return to Art 4(1) and the identification of the country with which the contract is most closely connected

The party who is to effect the characteristic performance

Once the characteristic performance is identified this performance must be connected to a particular country. The Convention achieves this by anchoring the characteristic performance in the country to which the party who is to effect this performance is connected. Thus, in a contract for the sale of goods this party will be the seller and in a contract for the provision of services this party will be the service provider. If this party was acting in the course of his trade or profession then it is to be presumed that the country with which the contract is most closely connected is the country in which the principal place of business is situated or, where, under the terms of the contract, the performance is to be effected through a place of business other than the principal place of business, the country in which that other place of business is situated. If the party to effect the characteristic performance was not acting in the course of his trade or profession then it is to be presumed that the country with which the contract is most closely connected is that in which, at the time of the conclusion of the contract, he had his habitual residence or, where that party is a body corporate or unincorporate, its central administration.

Disregarding the presumption

Article 4(2) of the Convention applies subject to Art 4(5) which states that "Paragraph 2 shall not apply if the characteristic performance cannot be determined, and the presumptions in paragraphs 2, 3 and 4 shall be disregarded if it appears from the circumstances as a whole that the contract is more closely connected with another country". Accordingly, the Art 4(2) presumption of closest connection will not apply where either the characteristic performance cannot be determined or, even if the characteristic performance can be determined, the law thereby identified shall be disregarded if it appears from the circumstances as a whole that the contract is more closely connected with another country (this ability to disregard the identified law also applies to the presumptions contained in Art 4(3) and (4)).

Difficulties have arisen as to the identification of the circumstances in which it is appropriate to depart from the law identified under the presumption in favour of the law that is considered to be more closely connected to the contract. The leading Scots case on this issue is *Caledonia Subsea Ltd* v *Micoperi Srl* (2003), a case in which the business of the characteristic performer was situated in Scotland but the contract was to be performed in Egypt. It was held that Art 4(2) intended to accord a special significance to the place of business of the principal performer as the indicator of the country with which the contract had the closest connection, moving away from emphasising the place of performance, and that the presumption should not be disregarded unless, exceptionally, there was a clear preponderance of factors showing a closer connection with another country. Such a "clear preponderance of factors" did not exist in the present case and the presumption remained operative in order to identify Scots law as the applicable law.

In the English case of *Definitely Maybe (Touring) Ltd* v *Marek Lieberberg Konzertagentur GmbH (No 2)* (2001), the party effecting the characteristic performance of the contract had its principal place of business in England, with that performance being the provision of the English pop group, Oasis, to play two concerts in Germany. Thus, under the Art 4(2) presumption, the applicable law was identified as the law of England. However, it was held that the obligations of the other party to arrange and market the concerts had arisen in Germany, the country in which the concerts had taken place, and, in light of these facts, the country with which the contract was most closely connected for the purpose of Art 4(5) was actually Germany. In *Intercontainer Interfrigo SC (ICF)* v *Balkenende Oosthuizen BV* (2010), the Grand Chamber of the European Court held, when considering the operation of Art 4(5) to displace the presumption applicable to a contract for the carriage of goods under Art 4(4), that when it was clear from the circumstances as a whole that the contract was "more closely connected" with a country other than that determined on the basis one of the Art 4 presumptions, it was for the court to disregard that presumption and apply the law of the country with which the contract was most closely connected.

The Regulation

Article 4(1) of the Rome I Regulation contains much more precise and detailed rules in cases where the parties have not chosen the applicable law. In the two most common types of contracts, for the sale of goods and the provision of services, Art 4(1) takes the presumption under Art 4(2) of the Convention that the country most closely connected thereto will be that of the seller/service provider and turns this into a fixed rule. Thus, under the Regulation, a contract for the sale of goods shall be governed by the law of the country where the seller has his habitual residence (Art 4(1)(a)) and a contract for the provision of services shall be governed by the law of the country where the service provider has his habitual residence (Art 4(1)(b)). Article 19 provides clarity as to what is considered to be the habitual residence of both natural persons and companies and other bodies, corporate or incorporated. Articles 4(1)(c)–(h) provide rules for other specific types of contract.

Article 4(2) provides guidance as to the applicable law in circumstances where the contract is not covered by any of the Art 4(1) rules or, alternatively, the contract has elements that fall within more than one limb of Art 4(1). In such cases the contract shall be governed by the law of the country where the party required to effect the characteristic performance of the contract has his habitual residence. It is essential to the operation of Art 4(2) that, regardless of the fact that the contract either is not covered by any of the Art 4(1) rules, or is covered by more than one of these rules, the characteristic performance of the contract must be identifiable. If the characteristic performance cannot be identified then Art 4(2) will not apply and recourse must be had to Art 4(4).

Article 4(3) is the equivalent of Art 4(5) of the Convention in stating that "Where it is clear from all the circumstances of the case that the contract is manifestly more closely connected with a country other than that indicated in paragraphs 1 or 2, the law of that other country shall apply". The addition of the word "manifestly" would seem to be an attempt to ensure that the Art 4(3) exception will only be applicable in exceptional circumstances where a country other than that indicated under Art 4(1) or (2) is significantly more closely connected to the contract. The mere fact that the contract is to be performed in a place other than that identified under Art 4(1) or (2) will not, by itself, be sufficient to satisfy the"manifestly more closely connected" test. Recital (20) of the Regulation indicates that in deciding whether a contract is manifestly more closely connected with a country other than that indicated, account should be taken of, *inter alia*, whether the contract in question has a very close relationship with another contract or contracts.

Article 4(4) provides that where the law applicable cannot be determined under Art 4(1) or (2), the contract shall be governed by the law of the country with which it is most closely connected. This provision will apply only when the contract does not fall within one of the specific rules of Art 4(1), or falls within more than one of these rules with there being a lack of harmony as to the law identified under each separate rule, and no characteristic performance can be identified for the purposes of Art 4(2). As with Art 4(3), Recital (21) of the Regulation indicates that one relevant factor in determining the country with which the contract is most closely connected is whether the contract in question has a very close relationship with another contract or contracts.

SPECIFIC CONTRACTS

The Rome I Regulation provides bespoke provisions for the identification of the applicable law in relation to contracts of carriage (Art 5); consumer contracts (Art 6); insurance contracts (Art 7); and individual employment contracts (Art 8). The justification for these specific provisions is to be found in Recital (23) in which it is explained that where contracts are concluded with parties regarded as being weaker, those parties should be protected by conflict of law rules that are more favourable to their interests than the general rules.

Contracts of carriage

Article 4(4) of the 1980 Rome Convention provides a specific presumption applicable to contracts for the carriage of goods. A similar provision is to be found in Art 5 of the Regulation, which also regulates contracts for the carriage of passengers. As regards contracts for the carriage of goods, Art 5(1) of the Regulation provides that, in the absence of choice, the law applicable to such contracts shall be the law of the carrier's habitual residence, provided that the place of receipt, place of delivery, or the habitual residence of the consignor is also situated in that country. Failing this, the applicable law will be the law of the agreed place of delivery.

In the absence of choice, the law applicable to a contract for the carriage of passengers shall be the law of the country where the passenger has his habitual residence, provided that either the place of departure or the place of destination is situated in that country. Failing this, the law of the country where the carrier has his habitual residence shall apply. While this provision applies only in the absence of choice, it is important to note that parties do not have complete freedom of choice, with any choice of applicable law limited to those laws specified in Art 5(2).

Article 5(3) provides that, where no choice has been made by the parties and it is clear from the circumstances of the case that the contract is manifestly more closely connected with a country other than that indicated in Art 5(1) or (2), the law of that other country shall apply.

Consumer contracts

Article 5 of the Convention applies to certain consumer contracts (Art 5(1)) when such a contract is entered into in any of the circumstances described in Art 5(2). In such circumstances the consumer would be protected in one of two ways. First, where the parties have agreed an applicable law, that choice would remain as the underlying law of the contract but this choice would not deprive the consumer of the protection of the mandatory rules of the law of the country in which he has his habitual residence (Art 5(2)). Second, where the parties do not agree an applicable law, the presumptions and rules of Art 4 will be displaced in favour of the law of the country in which the consumer has his habitual residence.

These special protective rules were revised in the Rome I Regulation and are now found in Art 6. Article 6(1) defines the type of consumer contracts to which its provisions apply, namely contracts concluded by a natural person for a purpose which can be regarded as being outside his trade or profession (the consumer) with another person acting in the exercise of his trade or profession (the professional). As with the protective jurisdictional provisions of the Brussels I Regulation, if the contract has a dual purpose in that it is entered into partly for private purposes and partly for professional or trade purposes then it will not be a consumer contract unless the business use element is negligible (*Gruber* v *Bay Wa AG* (2006)). If a contract does come within the terms of Art 6(1) it will be governed by the law of the country where the consumer has his habitual residence, provided that the professional pursues his commercial or professional activities in the country where the consumer has his habitual residence or, by any means, directs such activities to that country or to several countries including that country, and the contract falls within the scope of such activities. The meaning of "directs such activities" is to be interpreted consistently with the Brussels I Regulation so that the mere accessibility of the professional's website in the country where the consumer has his habitual residence does not, by itself, constitute the directing of activities.

Article 6(2) preserves party autonomy by allowing parties to choose the law applicable to a contract which fulfils the requirements of Art 6(1) but this choice is limited in that it may not have the result of depriving the consumer of the protection afforded to him by provisions that cannot be derogated from by agreement by virtue of the law of the consumer's habitual residence. In other words, a choice of law will be effective but it will be subject to the non-derogable provisions of the law of the habitual residence of the consumer. Article 6(4) specifies a number of contracts to which Art 6(1) and (2) do not apply.

Insurance contracts

Insurance contracts were not the subject of special coverage under the Rome Convention, with the rules thereof only applicable to contracts of insurance where the risk is situated outside the Member States of the EU (Art 1(3)). The Convention did, however, apply to all contracts of reinsurance (Art 1(4)). In contrast, Art 7 of the Rome I Regulation does provide specific treatment of insurance contracts.

Article 7 applies to insurance contracts covering a "large risk" (as defined in Art 7(2)), whether or not the risk covered is situated in a Member State, and to all other insurance contracts covering risks inside the territory of a Member State. Contracts of reinsurance do not come within the terms of these bespoke provisions. An insurance contract covering a large risk is governed by the law chosen by the parties in accordance with Art 3. If the parties have not chosen the applicable law then the insurance contract will be governed by the law of the country where the insurer has his habitual residence. However, where it is clear from all the circumstances of the case that the contract is manifestly more closely connected with another country, the law of that other country shall apply (Art 7(2)). This is the same result as would be achieved if the general rules in Arts 3 and 4 were applicable.

In the case of an insurance contract other than a contract covering a large risk, in order to provide protection for the policy holder the ability of the parties to choose the applicable law is restricted to only those laws identified in Art 7(3). However, where the law chosen is either the law of any Member State where the risk is situated at the time of conclusion of the contract (Art 7(3)(a)); or the law of the country where the policy holder has his habitual residence (Art 7(3)(b)); or in a business-to-business insurance contract, where the risks insured against relates to activities in more than one Member State, the law of any of those States (Art 7(3)(e)), if the law of that Member State permits wider part autonomy then the parties may take advantage of that greater freedom in order to choose an applicable law permitted by that law. In the absence of choice, an insurance contract other than a contract covering a large risk shall be governed by the law of the Member State in which the risk is situated at the time of the conclusion of the contract, as defined by Art 7(6). For example, the risk under a contract for vehicle insurance is situated in the Member State in which the vehicle is registered. Article 7(4) applies where, under the law of a Member State, the insurance of a risk is compulsory, while Art 7(5) provides a rule applicable when a contract covers risks situated in more than one Member State.

Individual employment contracts

Article 6 of the Convention and Art 8 of the Regulation provide specific rules applicable to individual employment contracts. Although the provisions are not identical, they are very similar and will be interpreted in the same way (*Koelzsch* v *Luxembourg* (2012)). Under Art 8(1), the default rule is that an individual employment contract will be governed by the law chosen by the parties. This choice is restrained, however, by the fact that such a choice of law may not have the result of depriving the employee of the protection afforded to him by provisions that cannot be derogated from by agreement under the law that, in the absence of choice, would have been applicable elsewhere under Art 8. In other words, while the choice of law will be effective, it will be applied subject to the mandatory rules of the law which would have been identified under Art 8 in the absence of choice.

Where the law applicable to the individual employment contract has not been chosen by the parties, Art 8(2) provides that the contract shall be governed by the law of the country in which or, failing that, from which the employee habitually carries out his work in performance of the contract. The country where the work is habitually carried out shall not be deemed to have changed if the employee is temporarily employed in another country. If, for whatever reason, the law applicable cannot be determined under Art 8(2) then Art 8(3) states that the contract shall be governed by the law of the country where the place of business through which the employee is engaged is situated. Article 8(4) permits the application of the law of a country other than that identified under Art 8(2) or (3) when it appears from the circumstances as a whole that the contract is more closely connected with that other country.

CONSENT AND MATERIAL VALIDITY

Article 8(1) of the Convention and Art 10(1) of the Regulation provide that the existence and validity of a contract, or of any term of a contract, shall be determined by the law which would govern it under the applicable instrument if the contract or term were valid. This is sometimes called the "putative applicable law". According to the Giuliano–Lagarde Report, this provision was intended to cover all aspects of the formation of the contract "other than general validity" (p 28). This phrase is understood to mean that the respective article of each instrument is intended to cover any matter relating to formation of the contract which is not governed by the other provisions of the relevant instrument, ie those issues referred to as matters of essential validity under the common law.

Article 10(2) of the Regulation goes on to provide that a party, in order to establish that he did not consent, may rely upon the law of the country in which he has his habitual residence if it appears from the circumstances that it would not be reasonable to determine the effect of his conduct in accordance with the law specified in Art 10(1). A similar provision appears in Art 8(2) of the Convention but with slightly different wording. The reason for the inclusion of this discretionary power is to solve the problem that in certain legal systems the silence on the part of the offeree implies acceptance (Giuliano–Lagarde Report, p 28). In *Egon Oldendorff* v *Libera Corp* (1995) Mance J, as he then was, stated that application of Art 8(2) of the Convention should adopt a "dispassionate, internationally minded approach" (at 70).

FORMAL VALIDITY

Issues of formal validity are governed by Art 11 of the Regulation which is in similar terms to Art 9 of the Convention. "Form" is defined in the Giuliano–Lagarde Report as including "every external manifestation required on the part of a person expressing the will to be legally bound, and in the absence of which such expression of will would not be regarded as fully effective" (p 29). Article 11 favours formal validity by identifying a number of different laws by which formal validity may be tested, compliance with the requirements of any of which will ensure formal validity. The principal rule of Art 11(1) is that a contract concluded between persons who, or whose agents, are in the same country at the time of its conclusion is formally valid if it satisfies the formal requirements of the law which governs it in substance under the Regulation, or of the law of the country where it is concluded. Article 11(2) provides that a contract concluded between persons who, or whose agents, are in different countries at the time of its conclusion is formally valid if it satisfies the formal requirements of the law which governs it in substance under the Regulation, or of the law of either of the countries where either of the parties or their agent is present at the time of conclusion, or of the law of the country where either of the parties had his habitual residence at that time. Article 11(3) applies to "unilateral acts" intended to have legal effect relating to an existing or contemplated contract. Article 11(4) provides that the formal validity of consumer contracts shall be governed by the law of the country where the consumer has his habitual residence, while Art 11(5) supplies a special rule relating to the formal validity of contracts relating to immoveable property.

CAPACITY

Article 1(2)(a) excludes questions of legal capacity of natural persons from the scope of the Regulation but this is stated as being without prejudice to Art 13. This article, which is in almost identical terms to the earlier Art 11 of the Convention, states that "In a contract concluded between persons who are in the same country, a natural person who would have capacity under the law of that country may invoke his incapacity resulting from the law of another country, only if the other party to the contract was aware of that incapacity at the time of the conclusion of the contract or was not aware thereof as a result of negligence". This provision is very limited in its terms, in particular the fact that it only applies to natural persons and only when those persons are contracting in the same country. Less specific is the reference simply to an incapacity resulting from the law of "another country", with no further guidance being given as to how this other law should be identified.

SCOPE OF THE LAW APPLICABLE

Article 12(1) provides that the applicable law identified by the Regulation shall govern, in particular, matters of interpretation (Art 12(1)(a)); performance (Art 12(1)(b)); the consequences of a total or partial breach of obligations (Art 12(1)(c)); the various ways of extinguishing obligations, and prescription and limitation of actions (Art 12(1)(d)); and the consequences of nullity of contract (Art 12(1)(e)). The terms of Art 12(1) are almost identical to the equivalent Art 10(1) of the Convention. Article 12(2) (Art 10(2) of the Convention) goes on to state that in relation to the manner of performance and the steps to be taken in the event of defective performance, regard shall be had to the law of the country in which performance takes place.

RESTRICTIONS ON THE APPLICABLE LAW
Overriding mandatory provisions

Overriding mandatory provisions are provisions the respect for which is regarded as crucial by a country for safeguarding its public interests, such as its political, social or economic organisation, to such an extent that they are applicable to any situation falling within their scope, irrespective of the law otherwise applicable to the contract under the Regulation (Art 9(1)). This definition did not appear in the Convention but the concept of overriding mandatory provisions is the same in both instruments in that they are provisions that a legal system considers so important that they should be applied regardless of what the applicable law is under its private international law rules. Unlike the mandatory provisions considered earlier under Art 3(3) and (4), overriding mandatory provisions will apply both when the parties have made a choice as to the applicable law and also when the applicable law has been determined under the Regulation in the absence of choice.

Article 9(2) of the Regulation provides that "Nothing in this Regulation shall restrict the application of the overriding mandatory provisions of the law of the forum". The same effect, although worded differently, is achieved by Art 7(2) of the Convention. This means that the forum is free to apply the overriding mandatory provisions of its own law no matter what law is otherwise applicable to the contract. Examples of such overriding mandatory provisions in the United Kingdom can be found in the Employment Rights Act 1996, s 204(1), and the Unfair Contract Terms Act 1977, s 27(2).

Article 9(3) provides that effect may be given to the overriding mandatory provisions of the law of the country where the obligations arising out of the contract have to be or have been performed, insofar as those overriding mandatory provisions render the performance of the contract unlawful. The equivalent provision of the Convention, Art 7(1), was worded differently in that it was much broader in its scope in referring to the law of "another country" with which the situation has a "close connection". It was not given effect to in the United Kingdom and a number of other Member States. The provision of the Regulation is much more specific than its predecessor in that it is limited to the rules of the country of performance and only to those rules which make performance illegal. Further, even if these requirements are met, the decision to apply Art 9(3) remains a discretionary one ("effect *may* be given"). In deciding whether to exercise this discretion, Art 9(3) provides some guidance in instructing that regard shall be had to the nature and purpose of the overriding mandatory provisions of the place of performance and to the consequences of their application or non-application in the case before the court.

Public policy of the forum

Article 21 of the Regulation provides that "The application of a provision of the law of any country specified by this Regulation may be refused only if such application is manifestly incompatible with the public policy (*ordre public*) of the forum". This is practically identical to the wording of its predecessor in Art 16 of the Convention. For Art 21 to apply it is not the foreign provision in general which is opposed but its application in the particular case before the court. In *Duarte* v *Black & Decker Corp* (2007), Art 16 of the Convention was relied on to disregard a restrictive covenant governed by the law of Maryland in circumstances where the employee was working in England when he entered into the covenant, the job he wished to take up was based in England, and the covenant would be unenforceable under English law.

Essential Facts

- The rules applicable to choice of law in contract are governed by either the 1980 Rome Convention or the Rome I Regulation. The former applies to contracts concluded between 1 April 1991 and 16 December 2009; the latter to contracts concluded as from 17 December 2009.
- Article 3 of the Convention permits parties to choose the law applicable to their contract, subject to the mandatory provisions of Art 3(3) and (4). This choice may be express or implied.
- Article 4(1) of the Convention determines the applicable law in the absence of choice by providing that a contract will be governed by the law of the country with which it is most closely connected.
- Article 4(1) of the Regulation provides specific rules to identify the applicable law in the absence of choice in relation to different types of contracts.
- The applicable law identified under Art 4 of the Convention may be disregarded if the contract is more closely connected with another country (Art 4(5)). The Regulation requires that the contract be *manifestly* more closely connected with another country (Art 4(3)).
- Special provision is made under the Regulation for contracts of carriage (Art 5); consumer contracts (Art 6); insurance contracts (Art 7); and individual employment contracts (Art 8).
- Article 9 of the Regulation (Art 7 of the Convention) permits the application of the overriding mandatory provisions of both the forum and the place of performance notwithstanding the law otherwise applicable under the Regulation.

Essential Cases

Beximco Pharmaceuticals Ltd v Shamil Bank of Bahrain EC (2004): choice of the governing law is limited to the law of a country.
Emeraldian Ltd Partnership v Wellmix Shipping Ltd (2010): Art 3(3) of the Convention applies only when all elements relevant to the situation are located in a single country.
Caledonia Subsea Ltd v Micoperi Srl (2003): the Art 4(2) presumption of the Convention should only be displaced under Art 4(5) when there is a clear preponderance of factors showing a closer connection with another country.

6 CHOICE OF LAW IN NON-CONTRACTUAL OBLIGATIONS

The rules applicable to choice of law in non-contractual obligations are now found in Regulation (EC) No 864/2007 of the European Parliament and of the Council of 11 July 2007 on the law applicable to non-contractual obligations, commonly referred to as the "Rome II Regulation". This Regulation largely, but not entirely, replaces both the traditional common-law rules and the statutory regime introduced by the Private International Law (Miscellaneous Provisions) Act 1995. Accordingly, the majority of this chapter will consider the provisions of the Rome II Regulation but some mention will be made at the end of the chapter of both the common-law rules and the provisions of the 1995 Act.

ROME II REGULATION

Scope

The Rome II Regulation applies to events giving rise to damage occurring from 11 January 2009 (Arts 31 and 32, as interpreted by the ECJ in *Homawoo* v *GMF Assurances SA* (2012)). The Regulation applies in all Member States other than Denmark and the use of the term "Member State" in the Regulation means any Member State other than Denmark (Art 1(4)).

The material scope of the Regulation is stated positively in Art 1(1) in that it shall apply, in situations involving a conflict of laws, to non-contractual obligations in civil and commercial matters. The phrase "civil and commercial matters" is to be given the same meaning as under the Brussels I Regulation and the Rome I Regulation. Whether an obligation is considered to be "non-contractual" is to be understood as an autonomous concept (Recital (11)). The Regulation only covers certain non-contractual obligations, with Art 2(1) stating that, for the purposes of the Regulation, "damage" shall cover any consequence arising out of tort/delict, unjust enrichment, *negotiorum gestio* or *culpa in contrahendo*. The Regulation extends to anticipated events in that it applies to non-contractual obligations that are likely to arise (Art 2(2)), with any reference to an event giving rise to damage including events giving rise to damage that are likely to occur and references to damage including damage that is likely to occur (Art 2(3)).

The material scope of the Regulation is also stated negatively in Art 1(1) in that it expressly does not apply to revenue, customs or administrative matters or to the liability of the state for acts and omissions in the exercise of State authority (*acta jure imperii*). As with the phrase "civil and commercial matters", the reference to "revenue, customs or administrative matters" is to be interpreted in the same way across Brussels I, Rome I and Rome II. The exclusion of claims arising out of *acta jure imperii* includes claims against officials who act on behalf of the state and liability for acts of public authorities, including liability of publicly appointed office-holders (Recital (9)). The scope of the Regulation is also narrowed by the express exclusion of certain matters as detailed in Art 1(2) and (3). All matters excluded from the Regulation remain subject to either the common-law rules or the rules contained in the Private International Law (Miscellaneous Provisions) Act 1995.

Article 3 states that the law specified by the Regulation shall be applied whether or not it is the law of a Member State. The Rome II Regulation thus takes the same approach as the Rome I Regulation in adopting the principle of universal application by giving the same treatment to the law of a non-EU Member State as it does to the law of an EU Member State. A composite state, such as the United Kingdom, is not required to apply the Regulation to internal conflicts between the laws of different territorial units within that state (Art 25(2)). However, in the interests of simplicity and uniformity of application, the United Kingdom has opted to extend the rules of the Regulation to intra-UK conflicts (for Scotland, see the Law Applicable to Non-Contractual Obligations (Scotland) Regulations 2008 (SSI 2008/404).

Applicable law by choice

Under Art 14, the Rome II Regulation implements the principle of party autonomy by allowing parties to choose the law applicable to non-contractual obligations. This is similar in approach to the choice that is given to parties to choose the law applicable to contractual obligations under the Rome I Regulation but, as non-contractual obligations will not normally be contemplated in advance, Art 14(1)(a) permits an agreement to be entered into only after the event giving rise to the damage occurred, unless all parties are pursuing a commercial activity, in which case an agreement freely negotiated may be entered into before the event giving rise to the damage occurred (Art 14(1)(b)). The rationale behind the restriction contained in Art 14(1)(a) is a desire to protect a weaker party who may not understand the significance of agreeing a choice of law before the damage has occurred. This mirrors the protective approach taken to "choice of court" agreements in matters relating to insurance, consumer contracts and individual contracts of employment under the Brussels I Regulation.

Once the event giving rise to the damage has occurred it is assumed that even a weaker party will be able to determine the law applicable under the Regulation in the absence of choice and will therefore be able to make an informed decision as to which law best suits his interests. In contrast, a party pursuing a commercial activity is considered to be in a more informed position and therefore cognisant of the consequences of making such a choice before the event giving rise to the damage has occurred.

The choice, whether made before or after the event giving rise to the damage, must be either expressed or demonstrated with reasonable certainty by the circumstances of the case. This language is very similar to that found in Art 3(1) of both the 1980 Rome Convention and the Rome I Regulation and reference should be made to the discussion related to these provisions in the previous chapter. Parties do not benefit from complete freedom of choice under the Rome II Regulation, as Arts 6(4) and 8(3) provide that a choice of law may not be made in relation to non-contractual obligations arising out of an act of unfair competition or the infringement of intellectual property rights. More generally, the choice of the parties is also subject to both the mandatory rules of the country in which all the elements relevant to the situation at the time when the event giving rise to the damage occurs are located (Art 14(2)), and the mandatory rules of Union law where all the elements relevant to the situation at the time when the event giving rise to the damage occurs are located in one or more of the Member States and the parties have chosen a law other than that of a Member State (Art 14(3)). Again, these provisions mirror those discussed in the previous chapter in relation to the Rome I Regulation and reference should be made thereto.

Torts/delicts: applicable law

Article 4 of the Rome II Regulation contains a general rule applicable to torts/delicts. This general rule is then supplemented by a number of additional rules applicable to specific forms of delictual liability.

Article 4(1): the law of the country in which the damage occurs

Article 4(1) states that:

> "Unless otherwise provided for in this Regulation, the law applicable to a non-contractual obligation arising out of a tort/delict shall be the law of the country in which the damage occurs irrespective of the country in which the event giving rise to the damage occurred and irrespective of the country or countries in which the indirect consequences of that event occur".

This general rule, operative in the absence of choice and also subject to the determination of the applicable law elsewhere in the Regulation, thus identifies the *lex loci damni*, the law of the country in which the damage occurs, as the applicable law. Accordingly, in cases of personal injury or damage to property, the country in which the damage occurs should be the country where the injury was sustained or the property was damaged respectively.

The issue of multi-locality delicts was previously considered under the Brussels I Regulation where it was seen that the similar phrase in Art 5(3) of that instrument of "the place where the harmful event occurred or may occur" has been interpreted for jurisdictional purposes to include both the place where the damage occurred and the place of the event which gives rise to this damage. In contrast, as can clearly be seen from the terms of Art 4(1) of the Rome II Regulation, any reference to the law of this latter place is not competent for choice of law purposes. Article 4(1) also excludes reference to the law of the country or countries in which only the indirect consequences of the event giving rise to the damage occur. This reflects a similar approach to jurisdiction under the Brussels I Regulation and means that the law of a country in which an individual suffers consequential financial loss or a deterioration in his condition following an injury suffered in another country will not be applicable under this rule.

Article 4(2): common habitual residence

Where the person claimed to be liable and the person sustaining damage both have their habitual residence in the same country at the time when the damage occurs, Art 4(2) provides that the law of that country shall apply. Although described by Recital (18) as an "exception" to the general principle of the application of the *lex loci damni*, Art 4(1) is subservient to Art 4(2) and, if the circumstances of the latter are apparent, this will oust the application of the former. Article 23 of the Regulation defines the habitual residence of companies and other bodies, corporate or unincorporated, as the place of central administration or, where the event giving rise to the damage occurs, or the damage arises, in the course of operation of a branch, agency or any other establishment, the place where the relevant branch, agency or any other establishment is located (Art 23(1)). The habitual residence of a natural person acting in the course of his business activity is stated to be his principal place of business (Art 23(2)). The habitual residence of a natural person acting in a non-business capacity is left undefined.

Article 4(3): the law that is manifestly more closely connected

Under Art 4(3), where it is clear from all the circumstances of the case that the tort/delict is manifestly more closely connected with a country other than that indicated in Art 4(1) or (2), the law of that other country shall apply. This test is the same as that adopted in Art 4(3) of the Rome I Regulation and similar to that found in Art 4(5) of the 1980 Rome Convention, and reference should be made to the discussion of these provisions in Chapter 5. Some guidance is also given in Art 4(3) itself, as the second sentence thereof states that a manifestly closer connection with another country might be based in particular on a pre-existing relationship between the parties, such as a contract, that is closely connected with the tort/delict in question. As Art 4(3) is not subject to the restrictions found in Art 4(1), the operation of the "manifestly more closely connected" rule could result in the application of either the law of the country in which the event giving rise to the damage occurred or the law of the country in which the indirect consequences of that event occur. The operation of Art 4(3) could also facilitate the displacement of the law of the common habitual residence applicable under Art 4(2) by the law of the country in which the damage occurs if the latter is manifestly more closely connected to the delict than the former.

Torts/delicts: specific rules

After providing the general rule of Art 4, the Regulation goes on to detail a number of specific rules in Arts 5–9 for particular types of delictual liability. Recital (19) justifies the need for these bespoke provisions on the basis that the application of the general rule "does not allow a reasonable balance to be struck between the interests at stake".

Product liability

The rules of Art 5 are presented in the form of a "cascade" provision which operates without prejudice to Art 4(2). In other words, in the absence of a choice of law under Art 14, the law principally applicable to a non-contractual obligation arising out of damage caused by a product shall be the common habitual residence of the parties as identified in Art 4(2). If the parties do not share a common habitual residence then a series of connecting factors is provided in Art 5(1) to the effect that the law applicable to a non-contractual obligation arising out of damage caused by a product shall be (a) the law of the country in which the person sustaining the damage had his habitual residence when the damage occurred, if the product was marketed in that country; or, failing that, (b) the law of the country in which the product was acquired, if the product was marketed in that country; or, failing that, (c) the law of the country in which the damage occurred, if the product was marketed in that country. In many cases the law of marketing, acquisition, habitual residence and damage will probably coincide. If the person claimed to be liable could not reasonably foresee the marketing of the product, or a product of the same type, in the country the law of which is applicable under the cascade, the law applicable shall be the law of the country in which that person is habitual resident. Article 5(2) provides a "manifestly more closely connected" exception equivalent to that found in Art 4(3). The complexity of this provision is compounded further by difficult issues of interpretation, particularly as regards the word "marketed", which is not defined in the Regulation.

Unfair competition and acts restricting free competition

Article 6 applies to acts of unfair competition and acts restricting free competition – categories that are unknown to the Scots law of delict. Recital (21) states that the special rule of Art 6 is not an exception to the general rule in Art 4(1) but rather a "clarification" of it, with the focus remaining on the law of the country in which the damage occurs. As regards unfair competition, if such an act affects exclusively the interests of a specific competitor then the rules of Art 4 will be applicable (Art 6(2)). Where the effects of an act of unfair competition are more general in that they affect multiple competitors or the market as a whole then the law applicable will be the law of the country where competitive relations or the collective interests of consumers are, or are likely to be, affected (Art 6(1)).

Article 6(3)(a) provides that the law applicable to a non-contractual obligation arising out of a restriction of competition shall be the law of the country where the market is, or is likely to be, affected. Article 6(3)(b) applies to cases in which the market is, or is likely to be, affected in more than one country and allows the pursuer to base his claim in one law if the conditions of that article are met. Article 6(4) restricts party autonomy in requiring that the law applicable under Art 6 may not be derogated from by an agreement under Art 14. It should be noted that this restriction only applies when the applicable law is determined by Art 6, if an act of unfair competition affects exclusively the interests of a specific competitor then Art 6(2) directs that Art 4 is to apply, under the terms of which a choice of law will be permitted.

Environmental damage

Article 7 applies to environmental damage or damage sustained by persons or property as a result of such damage. What is to be understood as environmental damage is identified in Recital (24). In cases of environmental damage, Art 7 directs that the law applicable shall be the law determined pursuant to Art 4(1): the law of the country in which the damage occurs. However, in direct contrast to Art 4(1), Art 7 also allows the pursuer to base his claim on the law of the country in which the event giving rise to the damage occurred. Article 7 is thus consistent with the choice of jurisdiction given to the pursuer in relation to delictual claims under Art 5(3) of the Brussels I Regulation. The parties may also make an agreement as to the applicable law in terms of Art 14.

Infringement of intellectual property rights

Article 8(1) applies the principle of *lex loci protectionis* in providing that the law applicable to a non-contractual obligation arising from infringement of an intellectual property right shall be the law of the country for which protection is claimed. The term "intellectual property rights" is to be interpreted as including copyright, related rights, the *sui generis* right for the protection of databases and industrial property rights (Recital (26)). Article 8(2) provides that, in the case of a non-contractual obligation arising from an infringement of a unitary Community intellectual property right, the law applicable shall, for any question that is not governed by the relevant Community instrument, be the law of the country in which the act of infringement was committed. Article 8(3) limits party autonomy in declaring that the law applicable under this article may not be derogated from by an agreement between the parties.

Industrial action

No definition of "industrial action" is included in the Regulation and Recital (27) states that the exact concept of industrial action, such as strike action or lock-out, varies from one Member State to another and is governed by each Member State's internal rules. Article 9 provides that

> "Without prejudice to Article 4(2), the law applicable to a non-contractual obligation in respect of the liability of a person in the capacity of a worker or an employer or the organisations representing their professional interests for damages caused by an industrial action, pending or carried out, shall be the law of the country where the action is to be, or has been, taken."

Accordingly, if the matter falls within the scope of Art 9 then, in the absence of an agreement as to applicable law under Art 14, the default position is that the law of the common habitual residence of the parties will apply ("without prejudice to Art 4(2)"). If the parties do not share a common habitual residence then the law of the country where the action is to be, or has been, taken will be applicable. If the parties do share a common habitual residence then the law of this country must be applied to industrial actions and there is no possibility of displacing this law in favour of the law that is manifestly more closely connected to the delict.

Other non-contractual obligations

Chapter III of the Rome II Regulation provides special rules in circumstances where a non-contractual obligation arises out of unjust enrichment, *negotiorum gestio* or *culpa in contrahendo*.

Unjust enrichment

A substantial proportion of problems arising under the head of unjust enrichment relate to a pre-existing relationship (usually contractual), between the parties. Article 10(1) acknowledges this by providing that if a non-contractual obligation arising out of unjust enrichment, including payment of amounts wrongly received, concerns a relationship existing between the parties, such as one arising out of a contract or a tort/delict, that is closely connected with that unjust enrichment, it shall be governed by the law that governs that relationship. The applicable law of the unjust enrichment will thus be guided by the applicable law identified according to the Rome I Regulation (if the pre-existing relationship is contractual), or the other provisions of the Rome II Regulation (if the pre-existing relationship is delictual). This has the benefit that the entire legal situation will be governed by the same law.

Where the applicable law cannot be determined by reference to the underlying relationship between the parties, Art 10(2) provides the second rule in the cascade in that if the parties have their habitual residence in the same country when the event giving rise to unjust enrichment occurs, the law of the common habitual residence will be applicable. If there is no underlying relationship between the parties, nor do they share a common habitual residence, Art 10(3) directs that the applicable law will be the law of the country in which the unjust enrichment took place. In circumstances in which a claim of unjust enrichment has links to a number of countries it is thought that "the country in which the unjust enrichment took place" points towards the country of immediate enrichment of the defender.

In similar terms to Art 4(3), Art 10(4) allows for the displacement of the law otherwise indicated under Art 10 when it is clear from all the circumstances of the case that there is a country with which the non-contractual obligation arising out of unjust enrichment is manifestly more closely connected. In such circumstances the law of this country will be the applicable law. Reliance on Art 10(4) could lead to an entirely new law being identified or it could be used to disrupt the cascade by, for example, leading to an application of the law of the common habitual residence in place of the law governing the pre-existing relationship. It is important to note that the rules of Art 10 will apply only in the absence of an agreement as to the applicable law under Art 14.

Negotiorum gestio

Negotiorum gestio refers to the situation in which a person (the *gestor*) intervenes, without any authority, to manage the affairs of another (the *dominus*) who, temporarily or permanently, is unable to manage his own affairs, in circumstances in which it is reasonable to assume that authority would have been given had the situation rendered it possible to apply for it. A *gestor* is entitled to be reimbursed for any expenditure he has incurred, regardless of whether the *dominus* was ultimately enriched by his actions. In such circumstances Art 11 applies a similar cascade provision to that found in Art 10 in relation to unjust enrichment. Thus, the applicable law will be the law governing the pre-existing relationship between the parties (Art 11(1)); or, failing that, the law of the country of common habitual residence at the time of the event giving rise to the damage (Art 11(2)); or, failing that, the law of the country in which the act was performed (Art 11(3)). Article 11(4) operates in identical fashion to Art 10(4). The application of Art 11 can be avoided if the parties make an agreement as to the applicable law under Art 14.

Culpa in contrahendo

The concept of *culpa in contrahendo* refers to those rules of national legal systems concerning the standard of conduct required of parties in pre-contractual negotiations. Recital (30) states that the concept is to be given an autonomous meaning for the purposes of the Regulation, with the consequence that matters which may be treated as contractual in Scots law will be classified as *culpa in contrahendo* for the purposes of the Rome II Regulation. Recital (30) provides further guidance by stating that the Regulation concept of *culpa in contrahendo* includes the violation of the duty of disclosure and the breakdown of contractual negotiations. Article 12 covers only non-contractual obligations presenting a direct link with the dealings prior to the conclusion of a contract, whether or not the contract is actually concluded.

If a contract is concluded then difficulties may arise with regard to the precise boundary between what is pre-contractual (and therefore governed by Art 12 of the Rome II Regulation), and what is contractual (and therefore governed by the Rome I Regulation). Such difficulties are ameliorated by Art 12(1) which provides that the law applicable to non-contractual obligations arising out of dealings prior to the conclusion of a contract is the law that applies to the contract, or that would have applied to the contract had it been entered into. Accordingly, reference should be made to the terms of the Rome I Regulation considered in Chapter 5.

Article 12(2) is another cascade provision that applies when the applicable law cannot be determined under Art 12(1). In such circumstances the applicable law will be the law of the country in which the damage occurs, irrespective of the country in which the event giving rise to the damage occurred and irrespective of the country or countries in which the indirect consequences of that event occurred; or, where the parties have their habitual residence in the same country at the time when the event giving rise to the damage occurs, the law of that country. The applicable law identified under Art 12(2)(a) and (b) may be avoided under Art 12(2)(c) where it is clear from all the circumstances of the case that the law of another country is manifestly more closely to the situation. Article 12(2)(c) only applies within its own paragraph and cannot be relied upon to avoid the application of the law identified in Art 12(1). Finally, as with Arts 10 and 11, parties may subject a non-contractual obligation arising out of dealings prior to the conclusion of a contract to the law of their choice under Art 14.

Reach of the applicable law

Once the applicable law is identified, Art 15 of the Regulation provides a detailed, but non-exhaustive, list of the issues to which it will apply. Of particular note is Art 15(c) which states that the applicable law identified under the Regulation will govern the existence, the nature and the assessment of damage or the remedy claimed. This is significant as, prior to the entry into force of the Rome II Regulation, the choice of law rule relating to damages (whether at common law or under the Private International Law (Miscellaneous Provisions) Act 1995) was partly substantive and partly procedural in that the applicable law determined what heads of damage were available but the quantification of damages was considered to be a procedural matter and therefore governed by the law of the forum. This classification of the quantification of damages as a matter of procedure to be regulated by the law of the forum was confirmed by the House of Lords in *Harding* v *Wealands* (2006). The terms of Art 15(c) in that the applicable law shall govern the existence, the nature and the assessment of damage or the remedy claimed rejects this previous approach by applying the applicable law to both the identification of the heads of damage and the quantification of damages. This can be compared with the assessment of damages under the Rome I Regulation, the equivalent Art 12(1)(c) of which states that the applicable law shall govern, *within the limits of the powers conferred on the court by its procedural law*, the consequences of a total or partial breach of obligations, including the assessment of damages *insofar as it is governed by rules of law*. The italicised words limit the scope of the applicable law under the Rome I Regulation and are notable for their absence under the Rome II Regulation.

Limits on the reach of the applicable law

Three notable limits are placed on the applicable law in terms of Arts 16, 17 and 26. Article 16 provides that nothing in the Regulation shall restrict the application of the provisions of the law of the forum in a situation where they are mandatory irrespective of the law otherwise applicable to the non-contractual obligation. This is a similar provision to Art 9 of the Rome I Regulation and reference should be made to the discussion of that article in the previous chapter. It should be noted, however, that Art 16 contains no definition of overriding mandatory provisions (in contrast to Art 9(1) of the Rome I Regulation), nor does it make any allowances for the overriding mandatory provisions of a third state (Art 9(3) of the Rome I Regulation).

Article 17 requires that, in assessing the conduct of the person claimed to be liable, account shall be taken, as a matter of fact and insofar as is appropriate, of the rules of safety and conduct which were in force at the place and time of the event giving rise to the liability, even where the non-contractual obligation is governed by the law of another country. According to Recital (34), the term "rules of safety and conduct" should be interpreted as referring to all regulations having any relation to safety and conduct, including, for example, road safety rules in the case of an accident.

Article 26 states that the application of a provision of the law of any country specified by the Regulation may be refused only if such application is manifestly incompatible with the public policy (*ordre public*) of the forum. It is not sufficient that the foreign rule of law should appear to be contrary to public policy in general: the operation of Art 26 requires that the application of the rule in the particular case before the court be contrary to public policy. According to Recital (32), the application of a provision of the law designated by the Regulation which would have the effect of causing non-compensatory exemplary or punitive damages of an excessive nature to be awarded may, depending on the circumstances of the case and the legal order of the Member State of the court seised, be regarded as being contrary to the public policy of the forum.

CLAIMS FALLING OUTSIDE THE ROME II REGULATION

Where delictual actions fall outside the material or temporal scope of the Rome II Regulation reference must be made to the pre-existing Scottish choice of law rules. These divide into the traditional common-law rules and the statutory regime introduced by the Private International Law (Miscellaneous Provisions) Act 1995. Given the extensive scheme of applicable law introduced by the Regulation, and its extension to intra-UK cases, the significance of both the common law and the 1995 Act has been marginalised to a residual role focused on non-contractual obligations arising out of violations of privacy and rights relating to personality, including defamation, which are excluded from the scope of the Regulation by Art 1(2)(g).

The common law

The common-law rules remain relevant to defamation claims which are excluded from both the scope of the Rome II Regulation (Art 1(2)(g)) and the 1995 Act (s 13). The common law is based on the rule of double action-ability which requires regard to be paid to both the *lex loci delicti* (the law of the place where the delict occurred), and the *lex fori* (the law of the forum), where an action concerning a delict committed overseas is litigated in the United Kingdom. In Scotland, there is no concept of party autonomy at common law and the applicable law will be determined independently of the parties' intentions. As a result of the applicability of the double action-ability rule, an act committed outside Scotland will be actionable as a delict within Scotland only if it was actionable as a delict both by Scots law and by the *lex loci delicti*. The flexible exception to this rule that developed in England first to displace the *lex loci delicti* (*Boys* v *Chaplin* (1971)) and, later, to displace the *lex fori* (*Red Sea Insurance Co Ltd* v *Bouygues SA* (1995)) has never been embraced in Scotland and the strict application of the double actionability rule remains part of Scots law.

Private International Law (Miscellaneous Provisions) Act 1995

The exclusion of non-contractual obligations arising out of violations of privacy and rights relating to personality from the scope of the Regulation means that such claims remain governed in Scotland by the provisions of the Private International Law (Miscellaneous Provisions) Act 1995. The Act abolished the common-law requirement of double actionability for claims falling within its scope and provides in s 11 that the applicable law will be the law of the country in which the events constituting the delict in question occur (s 11(1)). In the case of a multi-locality delict, the applicable law is the law of the country in which the most significant element or elements of those events occurred (s 11(2)(c)). This general rule of s 11 is subject to displacement under s 12 if it appears, in all the circumstances, from a comparison between the significance of the factors which connect a delict with the country whose law would be the applicable law under the general rule and the significance of any factors connecting the delict with another country, that it is substantially more appropriate for the applicable law to be the law of the other country. In making this assessment, the court may take into account, in particular, factors relating to the parties, to any of the events which constitute the delict in question or to any of the circumstances or consequences of those events.

Essential Facts

- The rules applicable to choice of law in non-contractual obligations are found primarily in the Rome II Regulation but both the common law and the Private International Law (Miscellaneous Provisions) Act 1995 retain a residuary role.
- The key provisions of the Rome II Regulation are:
  - Art 4: the applicable law will be the *lex loci damni*, the law of the common habitual residence of the parties or the law manifestly more closely connected;
  - Arts 5–9: specific rules for certain types of delictual liability;
  - Arts 10–12: specific rules relating to claims of unjust enrichment, *negotiorum gestio* and *culpa in contrahendo*;
  - Art 14: party autonomy;
  - Arts 16, 17 and 26: limits on the applicable law.
- Under Art 15(c) the applicable law will govern both the identification of the heads of damage and the quantification of damages.
- The common-law rule of double actionability requires actionability under both Scots law and the *lex loci delicti*: there is no flexible exception to this rule in Scotland. This rule remains applicable to defamation claims.
- The Private International Law (Miscellaneous Provisions) Act 1995 identifies the *lex loci delicti* as the applicable law (s 11), subject to displacement by the substantially more appropriate law (s 12).

Essential Cases

Harding v Wealands (2006): the quantification of damages is a matter of procedure to be determined by the law of the forum.

Boys v Chaplin (1971): in England, the common-law rule of double actionability is subject to a flexible exception which will operate to displace an otherwise applicable law.

7 MARRIAGE AND CIVIL PARTNERSHIP

This chapter will consider the rules of private international law applicable to opposite-sex marriage, same-sex civil partnership and their international equivalents.

MARRIAGE

The general concept of marriage is recognised throughout the world, although the precise boundaries of the relationship vary considerably between jurisdictions. Scots law, at least for the time being, remains faithful to what is considered to be the classic definition of marriage given by Lord Penzance in *Hyde* v *Hyde and Woodmansee* (1865–69) that marriage is a voluntary union for life of one man and one woman to the exclusion of all others. In contrast, whereas Scotland considers marriage to be a monogamous institution, certain other countries adopt a polygamous definition of marriage under which the marital relationship is not restricted to two parties. Further, the restriction that marriage is between specifically one man and one woman has been abandoned in an ever-increasing number of countries in which marriage is now open to both opposite-sex and same-sex couples. More subtle differences also exist, such as the fact that parental consent is required in England and Wales (and other jurisdictions) for parties who have reached their 16th birthday but have not attained the age of 18 (Marriage Act 1949, s 3) – a restriction that is unknown in Scotland.

The challenge for private international law is to provide a coherent set of rules which reflect this international diversity while giving sufficient acknowledgement to the law, or laws, that can claim to have a legitimate interest in the marriage. Historically, all questions relating to the validity of a marriage were referred exclusively to the *lex loci celebrationis* – the law of the place where the marriage was celebrated. In a world with little international mobility, where in most cases an individual would marry in his or her country of domicile a fellow domiciliary thereof, such a simple rule could be applied with relative ease. However, the developing availability of international travel led to both the possibility of cross-border relationships and also provided an opportunity for aspirant spouses to marry in a jurisdiction to which they had little, if any, prior connection, possibly for the sole purpose of avoiding domiciliary restrictions. This latter point is highlighted in the case of *Brook* v *Brook* (1861) where a marriage was celebrated in Denmark between two English domiciliaries, a widower and the sister of his deceased wife. Such a marriage was at that time prohibited under the English law relating to prohibited degrees but valid according to the law of Denmark. When a question arose as to the validity of the marriage the House of Lords held that the marriage was invalid on the basis that the exclusive application of the *lex loci celebrationis* was no longer appropriate and, instead, this law should determine only the formalities of the marriage, with the essentials of the marriage, most notably those concerned with issues of capacity and consent, referred to the *lex domicilii*, the domiciliary law of each spouse at the time of the marriage.

Formal validity

Formal validity is concerned with the actual manner in which a marriage is celebrated and covers procedural aspects such as whether notice has to be given in advance and, if so, to whom; the form of the marriage ceremony; the identity of the celebrant; and the requirement for witnesses. Questions of formal validity follow the principle of *locus regit actum* (the place governs the act), with the result that whether any particular ceremony constitutes a formally valid marriage depends solely on the law of the place in which the ceremony is held (*Berthiaume* v *Dastous* (1930), per Lord Dunedin at 83). This was previously a rule of the common law but has now been placed on a statutory footing in Scotland by s 38(1) of the Family Law (Scotland) Act 2006, subject to the limited exceptions discussed below. Accordingly, any marriage celebrated in Scotland must comply with the terms of the Marriage (Scotland) Act 1977 irrespective of the fact that the parties may be resident elsewhere and have limited connections to Scotland. The opposite of this is also true in that two Scottish domiciliaries celebrating a marriage overseas must comply with the requirements of the local law and the celebration of a marriage in contravention of this law, but valid under Scots law, would be insufficient, subject to the highly specialised circumstances identified below. Formal validity will usually be tested at the date of the ceremony, although there may be exceptional circumstances in which a marriage formally invalid at the time of celebration is later validated by subsequent legislation of the *lex loci*, in which case a later date may be identified (*Starkowski* v *Att Gen* (1954)).

Identification of the lex loci celebrationis

In the majority of cases the identification of the *lex loci celebrationis* will be unproblematic but difficulties arise in circumstances where a marriage has been celebrated in a jurisdiction at a time when at least one of the parties thereto is present in a different jurisdiction. In *Apt* v *Apt* (1948) the

English Court of Appeal upheld a marriage celebrated by proxy in Argentina between a man domiciled and resident there and a woman domiciled and resident in England on the basis that proxy marriages were valid by Argentine law, which was considered to be the *lex loci celebrationis*.

In *C* v *City of Westminster Social and Community Services Department* (2008) the parties had purportedly entered into a marriage in Bangladesh at a time when the wife was present in that country while the husband was both domiciled and present in England but had allegedly participated in the marriage ceremony via telephone. The parties had reached an agreement that the *lex loci celebrationis* was Bangladesh and further analysis of this was not necessary for the disposal of the case. Thorpe LJ (at para 42) challenged this consensus in the Court of Appeal and recommended that the issue be considered in a future case. Similar circumstances arose in the Scottish case of *A* v *K* (2011), where a marriage purportedly took place by telephone between a woman of UK nationality resident in Edinburgh and a man who had a postal address in Pakistan but appeared to be resident in Dubai. The subsequent marriage "certificate" stated that the place of solemnisation was Pakistan. It was held by Lord Stewart that Pakistan was the sole place of celebration. This finding has been criticised by Crawford and Carruthers who have argued that in circumstances such as were apparent in these two cases there should be a recognition that there can be more than one place of celebration (see E B Crawford and J M Carruthers, "Dual locality events: marriage by telephone" 2011 29 SLT (News) 227).

Exceptions to the general rule

The rule contained in s 38(1) is subject to the Foreign Marriage Act 1892. This Act, as amended, provides that a marriage between parties, of whom at least one is a United Kingdom national, will, if solemnised in a foreign country in the manner prescribed in the Act, be as valid in law as if it had been solemnised in the United Kingdom, even if it does not comply with the *lex loci celebrationis*. Such marriages are commonly referred to as "consular marriages". Provision is also made in the 1892 Act, as amended, and the Foreign Marriages (Armed Forces) Order 1964 (SI 1964/1000) for the solemnisation of marriages in a foreign territory between parties at least one of whom is a member of the armed forces. As with consular marriages, a marriage celebrated in the manner prescribed will be as valid in law as if it had been solemnised in the United Kingdom, even if the *lex loci celebrationis* has not been complied with. Further exceptions exist under English common law where the use of local form is impossible or the marriage takes place in a country under belligerent occupation. Following the statutory codification of the common-law rule, and the reference therein to only the 1892 Act, these exceptions are no longer applicable in Scotland.

Capacity to marry

Capacity to marry is concerned with issues such as the acceptable degrees of affinity or consanguinity and the minimum age at which a party may marry. A number of different arguments have been advanced to identify the most appropriate law to govern these issues of capacity, with support for the law of the ante-nuptial domicile(s) of the parties, the law of the intended matrimonial home and the law of the jurisdiction with which the marriage has its most real and substantial connection finding at least some degree of support from both the judiciary and in academic writings. It is the first of these alternatives which has received most support and this has now been recognised in Scotland with the common-law rule receiving statutory endorsement in s 38(2) of the Family Law (Scotland) Act 2006. This section implements what is commonly known as the "dual domicile rule" in providing that a person's capacity to enter into a marriage shall be determined by the law of the place where, immediately before the marriage, that person was domiciled. It is important to note that the dual domicile rule is one of cumulative application in that, should the parties not share the same domicile, each party must have legal capacity to marry according to their own *lex domicilii*. An impediment to marriage existing under the law of the domicile of just one of the parties may invalidate the marriage irrespective of the fact that all other relevant laws are satisfied. Subject to the exceptions noted below, it is now the position in Scotland that the dual domicile rule must be applied to determine issues of capacity and reference to any alternative rule, such as may still occur in England, even if such alternative would uphold the validity of an otherwise invalid marriage, is no longer competent.

Exceptions to the general rule

The general rule of s 38(2) is subject to three exceptions. First, under s 38(3), if a marriage entered into in Scotland is void under a rule of Scots domestic law, then the Scots rule shall prevail over the domiciliary rule under which the marriage would be valid. This exception protects the fundamental principles of the domestic understanding of marriage by applying the mandatory rules of Scots law as regards capacity to marry to all marriages celebrated within Scotland, irrespective of the domicile of the parties. For example, regardless of the terms of the domiciliary laws of the parties, a marriage celebrated in Scotland will be void if either party is under 16 or within the forbidden degrees of relationship as stated in ss 1 and 2 of the Marriage (Scotland) Act 1977 respectively. It should be noted that s 38(3) operates only in the negative sense in that it will invalidate an otherwise valid marriage; it does not apply positively in order to validate a marriage otherwise invalid under the domiciliary laws of the parties. Further, s 38(3) and its reference to the laws of the *lex loci celebrationis* only applies to marriages celebrated in Scotland and the 2006 Act is silent with regard to the question of whether capacity should also be required by a foreign *lex loci celebrationis*.

Second, s 38(4) permits a derogation from the general rule when a reference to the *lex domicilii* would be contrary to Scottish public policy. Unlike s 38(3), this section may operate both positively and negatively and contains no geographical boundary. It could operate to ignore an objectionable domiciliary impediment to marriage, such as restrictions based on race or religion. Conversely, an otherwise valid marriage might be refused recognition because of an objectionable capacity, such as the ability under the *lex domicilii* to marry at a very young age or to marry a closely related person (*Cheni* v *Cheni* (1965)).

Finally, the general rule must defer to s 50 of the Family Law Act 1986 which provides that where a divorce or annulment is either granted or recognised in any part of the United Kingdom, the fact that this divorce or annulment would not be recognised elsewhere shall not preclude either party to the marriage from re-marrying in the United Kingdom or cause the re-marriage of either party (wherever the re-marriage takes place) to be treated as invalid in the United Kingdom.

As with matters of formal validity, the statutory restatement of both this choice of law rule and its exceptions now precludes any reference to exceptions found under the common law. Accordingly, the much-criticised rule of English law under which a marriage celebrated in England, between parties of whom one has an English domicile and the other a foreign domicile, will be valid even if an incapacity exists under the domiciliary law of the other party, is no longer part of the law of Scotland, if it ever was (*Sottomayor* v *De Barros (No 2)* (1879)).

Consent to marry

While the method of giving consent is a matter for the *lex loci celebrationis*, there was previously some doubt as to the law applicable to the question of whether a party gave true consent to a marriage (compare *Di Rollo* v *Di Rollo* (1959) with *Singh* v *Singh* (2005)). This doubt was removed by s 38(2) of the Family Law (Scotland) Act 2006 which treats consent in the same way as capacity by referring the determination of this issue to the law of the ante-nuptial domicile, subject to the aforementioned exceptions. If the marriage is celebrated in Scotland then s 20A of the Marriage (Scotland) Act 1977 states that a marriage will be void if a party to the marriage who was capable of consenting to the marriage purported to give consent but did so by reason only of duress or error, the latter being defined in s 20A(5). A marriage will also be void if at the time of the marriage ceremony a party to the marriage was incapable of understanding the nature of marriage and consenting to the marriage. Further, under s 20A(4), if a party to a marriage purported to give consent to the marriage other than by reason only of duress or error, the marriage shall not be void by reason only of that party's having tacitly withheld consent to the marriage at the time when it was solemnised.

The question as to whether the issue of parental consent to marriage was one of formal validity, referable to the *lex loci celebrationis*, or an element of essential validity, referable to the law of the ante-nuptial domicile, also caused some difficulty in the past (see *Ogden* v *Ogden* (1908) and *Bliersbach* v *McEwen* (1959)). This issue is now governed by s 38(5) of the Family Law (Scotland) Act 2006 which states that if the law of the place in which a person is domiciled requires a person under a certain age to obtain parental consent before entering into a marriage, that requirement shall not be taken to affect the capacity of a person to enter into a marriage in Scotland unless failure to obtain such consent would render invalid any marriage that the person purported to enter into in any form anywhere in the world.

Polygamous marriages

Polygamous marriages are marital unions involving more than two spouses, usually because a legal system permits a husband to take multiple wives. While domestic conceptions of marriage as a monogamous institution prevent the formation of such marriages within Scotland (Marriage (Scotland) Act 1977, s 5(4)(b)), questions have arisen regarding the recognition of marriages formed under a law which does permit polygamy. Originally, the response to such marriages, based upon an arguably mistaken interpretation of the judgment of Lord Penzance in *Hyde* v *Hyde and Woodmansee* (1865–69), was that marriages formed under a law which permits polygamy should not be recognised at all, regardless of whether the marriage was potentially or actually polygamous, ie recognition would be refused to all marriages formed under a polygamous system of law, even if the marriage was in reality monogamous. This aversion towards such marriages was gradually relaxed through a growing realisation that recognition could be given not in general but for particular purposes, such as the granting of matrimonial relief. This approach was placed on a statutory footing by s 2 of the Matrimonial Proceedings (Polygamous Marriages) Act 1972 which provides that the fact that a marriage was entered into under a law which permits polygamy shall not preclude the Scottish courts from entertaining proceedings for, or granting, specified matrimonial decrees. The 1972 Act was also significant in that it reduced the importance of the distinction between potentially and actually polygamous marriages. This Act was followed by s 7(2) of the Private International Law (Miscellaneous Provisions) Act 1995 which confirms that all potentially polygamous marriages will, so long as neither party marries a second spouse during the subsistence of the marriage, have the same effects for all purposes of the law of Scotland as a monogamous marriage.

Capacity to enter into a polygamous marriage

As with monogamous marriage, capacity to enter into a polygamous marriage is governed by the law of the ante-nuptial domicile. Accordingly, if parties to a marriage which is actually polygamous have their domiciles in a country (or countries) which permit polygamy, and they comply with all the formal requirements of the *lex loci celebrationis*, this marriage can be recognised in Scotland. In contrast, an actually polygamous marriage celebrated overseas in contravention of a monogamous domiciliary law will not be recognised. A Scottish domiciliary is thus prevented from entering an *actually* polygamous marriage but any marriage that such an individual enters into under a polygamous system of law will still be recognised as a valid marriage if it is *potentially* polygamous but in reality monogamous (s 7(2) of the Private International Law (Miscellaneous Provisions) Act 1995).

CIVIL PARTNERSHIP

Alongside opposite-sex marriage a number of jurisdictions have chosen to provide legal recognition to same-sex couples through either the provision of a functional equivalent to marriage (Denmark being the first to do so in 1989) or the opening up of marriage itself (the Netherlands being the first to do so in 2001). The United Kingdom at present adopts the former approach (though moves to permit the latter are under way) and since December 2005 has permitted the registration of civil partnerships in accordance with the provisions of the Civil Partnership Act 2004. Part 3 of the 2004 Act governs civil partnerships registered in Scotland while Pt 5 provides detailed private international law provisions relating to the formation of same-sex relationships overseas and the subsequent recognition of such relationships in Scotland (and the rest of the United Kingdom).

Civil partnerships registered in Scotland

If a civil partnership is to be registered in Scotland a cumulative reading of ss 1, 85 and 86 of the 2004 Act reveals that both the formation of the civil partnership and the eligibility (a term used in place of "capacity") of the parties to enter the relationship will be determined exclusively by the domestic rules of Scots law. Any reference to the parties also requiring eligibility/capacity under their ante-registration domicile is notable by its absence. Accordingly, if a civil partnership is registered in Scotland (or in any other part of the United Kingdom) then, regardless of the domicile of the parties thereto, the *lex loci registrationis*, the law of the place of registration, will determine all questions of validity, whether formal or essential.

Same-sex relationships formed overseas

Questions regarding the validity of a same-sex relationship formed overseas are governed by s 215 of the 2004 Act which provides a general rule that matters of both capacity and formal validity are to be referred to the "relevant law", which is defined under s 212(2) as the law of the country or territory where the relationship is registered (including its rules of private international law). The *lex loci registrationis*, or the *lex loci celebrationis* in the case of a same-sex marriage, is therefore pre-eminent in determining issues of both formal and essential validity. As with registrations taking place in Scotland, there is no explicit reference to domiciliary law, with the consequence that the 2004 Act in effect provides a statutory codification of an approach deemed unsuitable for opposite-sex marriage over 150 years ago following the decision in *Brook* v *Brook* (1861). The reason for this different approach can be found in the still-limited international acceptability of legally formalised same-sex relationships. To refer the issue of capacity to enter a same-sex relationships to the *lex domicilii* would, even in light of the growing number of jurisdictions granting recognition to such relationships, invariable identify a law which had no concept thereof and was therefore silent as to capacity to enter such a relationship. Instead, by referring the question of capacity to the law of registration/celebration this issue has been avoided, although it does create a different issue of "limping relationships" which will be recognised in some jurisdictions, notably the place of registration/celebration and Scotland, but potentially not by the law of the domicile of the parties thereto.

For an overseas same-sex relationship to be recognised in Scotland not only must the parties themselves satisfy the terms of the 2004 Act but their chosen relationship form must also comply with the characterisation requirements of the 2004 Act. These requirements can be found in ss 212 and 214 which specify that an overseas relationship will be recognised only if it requires registration, is sanctioned by the state, is monogamous and between parties of the same sex whom, upon registration, will be treated as a couple either generally or for specified purposes, or treated as married, for an indeterminate duration. Schedule 20 provides a statutory list of those specified relationships which are considered to fulfil this criteria without further investigation (this list was updated on 31 January 2013 by the Civil Partnership Act 2004 (Overseas Relationships) Order 2012 (SI 2012/2976)). The requirement that an overseas relationship will only be recognised when the parties are of the same sex prevents the recognition under the 2004 Act of those overseas non-marital relationships, such as are available in, for example, Belgium, France, the Netherlands and New Zealand, registered between two parties of the opposite sex.

If a relationship is to be recognised in Scotland then s 215 provides that the parties thereto will be "treated as having formed a civil partnership". This method of equating the varying forms of same-sex relationship recognition available around the world with a domestic civil partnership has the benefit of simplicity but may also lead to two divergent problems. First, individuals party to an overseas relationship with more limited legal consequences, such as the Belgian relationship of *cohabitation légale*, will automatically be attributed with a more onerous range of rights and obligations. In contrast, those individuals party to an overseas same-sex marriage may consider that their relationship has been downgraded by being recognised not as a marriage but as a civil partnership (*Wilkinson* v *Kitzinger* (2006)).

Exceptions to the general rule

There are three exceptions to the general rule that the law of registration/celebration will determine all issue of validity. First, and replicating the provisions applicable to opposite-sex marriage, s 210 of the 2004 Act permits the registration of a civil partnership at a British Consulate in accordance with the law of a part of the United Kingdom that the parties have chosen to apply in preference to the law of the place where the consulate is situated. Second, and once again reflecting the approach to opposite-sex marriage, s 211 provides for the registration of a civil partnership according to the law of a part of the United Kingdom when at least one of the parties is a member of the armed forces. Finally, s 217 permits a residual role for the law of domicile when a relationship is entered into overseas if that relationship involves at least one party who is domiciled in a part of the United Kingdom. This section will extend all domestic domiciliary incapacities to any such overseas registration and would prevent, for example, an individual domiciled in Scotland evading the Scottish rules as to consanguinity or nonage by registering a partnership abroad.

Essential Facts

Marriage

- Validity of an opposite-sex marriage is determined according to s 38 of the Family Law (Scotland) Act 2006, with matters of formal validity referred to the *lex loci celebrationis* and matters of essential validity (notably capacity to marry) referred to the *lex domicilii*.
- Exceptions to the above are entirely statutory and are to be found in s 38(1) as regards formal validity and s 38(2), (3) and (4) as regards essential validity. Previous common-law exceptions are no longer applicable.
- Polygamous marriages, both potentially and actually polygamous, will now be recognised in Scotland for most purposes (Matrimonial Proceedings (Polygamous Marriages) Act 1972, s 2, and Private International Law (Miscellaneous Provisions) Act 1995, s 7).

Civil partnership

- If a civil partnership is registered in Scotland then Scots law will determine issues of both form and eligibility (Civil Partnership Act 2004, ss 1, 85 and 86).
- The law of the country or territory where an overseas relationship is registered (including its rules of private international law) will be applied to all issues of validity under s 215 of the 2004 Act, subject to the exceptions found in ss 210, 211 and 217.
- All overseas same-sex relationships will be recognised in Scotland as civil partnerships.

Essential Cases

Hyde v Hyde and Woodmansee (1865–69): provides the classic definition of marriage as "the voluntary union for life of one man and one woman, to the exclusion of all others". This definition was relied upon initially to prevent the recognition of polygamous marriages.

Brook v Brook (1861): the formal validity of a marriage is determined by the *lex loci celebrationis* (the law of the place where the marriage takes place), but the essentials of the marriage, most notably concerned with issues of capacity and consent, will be referred to the *lex domicilii* (the law of the ante-nuptial domicile of each party).

A v K (2011): where a marriage by telephone between a woman in Scotland and a man purportedly present in Pakistan was stated on the marriage certificate as having been celebrated in Pakistan, the *lex loci celebrationis* was held to be the law of Pakistan.

Wilkinson v Kitzinger (2006): an overseas same-sex marriage will be recognised in the United Kingdom as a civil partnership.

8 DIVORCE AND DISSOLUTION

This chapter will consider the private international law rules applicable to the dissolution of those formalised personal relationships considered in Chapter 7, primarily opposite-sex marriage. These rules first developed through the common law before later being subject to statutory codification and, more recently, they have become the focus of a number of European harmonisation initiatives. Issues of jurisdiction, choice of law and recognition will each be considered in turn.

JURISDICTION

The Domicile and Matrimonial Proceedings Act 1973 created a new set of jurisdictional principles which replaced the law in force prior to 1 January 1974. This Act provided that the Court of Session would have jurisdiction to entertain an action for divorce if either of the parties to the marriage was domiciled in Scotland on the date the action was begun, or, had been habitually resident in Scotland throughout the period of 1 year ending with that date (s 7). These rules remained in place until 1 March 2001 when Council Regulation (EC) No 1347/2000 of 29 May 2000 on jurisdiction and the recognition and enforcement of judgments in matrimonial matters and in matters of parental responsibility for children of both spouses (commonly referred to as the "Brussels II Regulation") came into force. This Regulation introduced a new set of uniform jurisdictional rules in matrimonial matters and facilitated the almost automatic recognition of matrimonial judgments throughout the European Union, with the exclusion of Denmark. The Brussels II Regulation was quickly revised and replaced by Council Regulation (EC) No 2201/2003 of 27 November 2003 concerning jurisdiction and the recognition and enforcement of judgments in matrimonial matters and matters of parental responsibility, repealing Regulation (EC) No 1347/2000 (commonly referred to as the "Brussels IIa Regulation"). The Brussels IIa Regulation incorporates the provisions relating to matrimonial matters found in the earlier Brussels II Regulation with no significant alterations, although it does expand the provisions relating to parental responsibility which will be considered in Chapter 11. From 1 March 2005, the Brussels IIa Regulation became directly applicable in all EU Member States, once again excluding Denmark.

Following the entry into force of the Brussels IIa Regulation the Scottish jurisdictional rules are now contained in the amended s 7(2A) of the 1973 Act to the effect that the Court of Session will have jurisdiction to entertain an action for divorce or separation if (and only if) the Scottish courts have jurisdiction under the Regulation, or, the action is an excluded action and either of the parties to the marriage is domiciled in Scotland on the date when the action is begun. Section 7(2A) thus identifies both the primary grounds of jurisdiction, those available under the Regulation, and a single residual ground of jurisdiction applicable when the action is an "excluded" action. Section 8 provides further rules granting jurisdiction to the sheriff courts if certain localising criteria are met.

Primary grounds of jurisdiction

Article 3 of the Brussels IIa Regulation sets out seven jurisdictional bases. The order in which they appear in the article is immaterial as there is no hierarchy and all grounds have an equal status and exclusive effect. Article 3(1) provides that, in matters relating to divorce, legal separation or marriage annulment, jurisdiction shall lie with the courts of the Member State:

  (a) in whose territory:
    i.   the spouses are habitually resident, or
    ii. the spouses were last habitually resident, insofar as one of them still resides there, or
    iii. the respondent is habitually resident, or
    iv. in the event of a joint application, either of the spouses is habitually resident, or
    v.   the applicant is habitually resident if he or she resided there for at least a year immediately before the application was made, or
    vi. the applicant is habitually resident if he or she resided there for at least six months immediately before the application was made and is either a national of the Member State in question or, in the case of the United Kingdom and Ireland, has his or her "domicile" there;
  (b) of the nationality of both spouses or, in the case of the United Kingdom and Ireland, of the "domicile" of both spouses.

Priority has been afforded in Art 3 to the connecting factor of habitual residence, utilised in a number of different circumstances, but there remains a role for the traditional connecting factors of nationality and domicile. This is particularly so in Art 3(1)(b) through which jurisdiction can be founded on the basis of joint nationality/domicile regardless of where the spouses are habitually resident. Where spouses each have dual nationality in the same Member States, Art 3(1)(b) gives the courts of either of those states jurisdiction to hear matrimonial proceedings and the spouses can seise a court in the Member State of their choice (*Hadadi* v *Mesko* (2009)). Article 3(1)(a)(iv) is not applicable in Scotland. Articles 4 and 5 provide two further ancillary grounds of jurisdiction, relating to counterclaims and conversions respectively.

Article 3(2) provides that, for the purposes of the Regulation, "domicile" shall have the same meaning as it has under the legal systems of the United Kingdom and Ireland. In other words, the Regulation adopts the 'traditional' definition of domicile and reference should be made to the discussion of this concept found in Chapter 2. In contrast, "habitual residence" is to be given an autonomous meaning for the purposes of the Brussels IIa Regulation – a meaning that will not necessarily be the same as the UK domestic meaning, nor the same as the meaning ascribed to the concept in other instruments. Habitual residence under the Regulation is meant to identify the place where an individual has established, on a fixed basis, his permanent or habitual centre of interests. In *Marinos* v *Marinos* (2007), Munby J held that for the purposes of the Regulation a person can have only one habitual residence – a finding that is directly at odds with the interpretation given to the domestic understanding of habitual residence for the purposes of divorce jurisdiction in the case of *Ikimi* v *Ikimi (Divorce: Habitual Residence)* (2001). In *Marinos*, Munby J also considered the meaning of "resided" for the purposes of Art 3(1)(a)(v) and (vi) and whether this was to be understood as requiring habitual residence for the requisite period, or some lesser form of residence. Munby J believed the latter was the correct interpretation and that only residence *simpliciter* need be established. This view was, however, challenged by Bennett J in *Munro* v *Munro* (2007) and it is yet to be settled definitively.

Residual ground of jurisdiction

Aside from jurisdiction under the Regulation, the Scottish courts will also have jurisdiction under s 7(2A) of the 1973 Act, if the action is an excluded action and either of the parties to the marriage is domiciled in Scotland on the date when the action is begun. To understand what is meant by an excluded action it is necessary to refer to Arts 6 and 7. Article 6 states that a spouse who is habitually resident in the territory of a Member State, or a national of a Member State, or, in the case of the United Kingdom and Ireland, has his or her domicile in the territory of one of these two Member States, may be sued in another Member State only in accordance with Art 3 (or in accordance with the ancillary jurisdictional grounds of Arts 4 and 5). Article 6 thus requires that a spouse with a connection to a Member State, whether through habitual residence, nationality or domicile, may only be sued in another Member State if the courts of that other state have jurisdiction under Art 3. Consequently, the Scottish residual jurisdictional ground of sole domicile may not be utilised by a "Scottish" spouse as against a spouse who is "European" in the sense of Art 6, whether or not that spouse is currently living in the European Union. It is only when a spouse is not "European" that a Scottish court *may* be able to utilise the residual ground of jurisdiction. However, Art 6 must be read in conjunction with Art 7(1) which provides that where no court of a Member State has jurisdiction pursuant to Art 3 (or Arts 4 and 5), jurisdiction shall be determined, in each Member State, by the laws of that state. Accordingly, the Scottish ground of residual jurisdiction will become effective only when, first, the respondent spouse is not "European" in terms of Art 6, and, second, no other court is capable of claiming jurisdiction under the Regulation (Art 7). These two requirements are cumulative and both must be satisfied before recourse may be had to the residual ground of jurisdiction (*Sundelind Lopez* v *Lopez Lizazo* (2007)).

Conflicts of jurisdiction

With such broadly drawn jurisdictional rules it is quite possible that spouses may be able to bring matrimonial proceedings in the courts of more than one country. For example, under the Regulation a married Italian couple living in Scotland would be able to bring proceedings in both Italy (joint nationality: Art 3(1)(b)) and Scotland (joint habitual residence: Art 3(1)(a)(i)) The solution adopted by the Scottish courts *vis-à-vis* such conflicts of jurisdiction will depend upon whether jurisdiction has been taken under the Regulation or via the residual ground of jurisdiction.

Lis pendens

The Brussels IIa Regulation follows the approach of the Brussels I Regulation when allocating jurisdiction between competing legal systems by implementing a "first come, first served" rule of strict priority. Accordingly, Art 19 provides that, where proceedings relating to divorce, legal separation or marriage annulment between the same parties are brought before courts of different Member States, the court second seised shall of its own motion stay its proceedings until such time as the jurisdiction of the court first seised is established (Art 19(1)). Once the jurisdiction of the court first seised is established, the court second seised shall decline jurisdiction in favour of that court (Art 19(3)). This applies when proceedings are brought between the same parties, even if the precise cause of action may differ. Article 16 provides clarity as regards when a court shall be deemed to be seised.

Mandatory sists

As Art 19 refers to proceedings being brought before the courts of different Member States, conflicts wholly internal to the United Kingdom continue to be governed by the system of mandatory sists regulated by Sch 3, para 8 to the 1973 Act. If the four conditions contained in para 8 are satisfied then a Scottish court must sist the action before it in favour of the courts in a "related jurisdiction", ie courts elsewhere in the British Isles as defined by Sch 3, para 3. The intention behind this provision is to ensure that the case is heard in the courts of the country in which the parties had their last, or most recent, matrimonial residence and, due to their mandatory nature, there is little practical difference between the application of Art 19 of the Regulation and Sch 3, para 8 to the 1973 Act.

Discretionary sists

Paragraph 9(1) of Sch 3 to the 1973 Act makes provision for a consistorial action to be sisted, before the beginning of the proof, whether in the Court of Session or a sheriff court, if it appears that any other proceedings in respect of the marriage in question or capable of affecting its validity are continuing in another jurisdiction and that the balance of fairness (including convenience) as between the parties to the marriage is such that it is appropriate for those other proceedings to be disposed of before further steps are taken in the action in the Scottish court. In considering the balance of fairness and convenience the court is required to have regard to all factors appearing to be relevant, including the convenience of witnesses and any delay or expense which may result from the proceedings being sisted, or not being sisted (Sch 3, para 9(2)). In *De Dampierre* v *De Dampierre* (1988) it was established that this terminology was the statutory equivalent of the doctrine of *forum non conveniens* and that the approach taken to the latter was equally applicable to the former. Further detail regarding this approach can be found in Chapter 3 but, in short, before the court will exercise its discretion under para 9(1) the respondent in the divorce proceedings will have to show that that there is another available forum which, *prima facie*, is clearly more appropriate. If successful in this plea, a sist will be granted unless the petitioner can show circumstances by reason of which justice requires that a sist should nevertheless not be granted. It is not enough for the petitioner simply to point to the loss of a legitimate personal or juridical advantage if required to litigate abroad.

While Art 19 will apply if jurisdiction is taken under the Regulation, the option to sist an action under Sch 3, para 9 remains available when proceedings have been brought in Scotland under the residual jurisdictional ground of the Scottish domicile of either spouse. However, as with the

Brussels I Regulation, questions have arisen as to whether a court in the United Kingdom which takes jurisdiction under the Regulation may sist an action in favour of a court in a country outside of the European Union. These questions are answered clearly in Scotland by s 11(2) of the 1973 Act which states that the power to sist an action is "subject to Article 19". Thus, in Scotland, once jurisdiction is taken under the Regulation the *lis pendens* approach to competing jurisdictions must be followed and a discretionary sist will not be competent. The situation is less clear in England, however, and in the case of *JKN* v *JCN* (2010) proceedings taken under Art 3 were stayed under the equivalent English provisions (1973 Act, Sch 1, para 9) in favour of New York.

Civil partnership

The jurisdictional rules relating to civil partnerships are detailed in ss 219 and 225 of the Civil Partnership Act 2004, and the Civil Partnership (Jurisdiction and Recognition of Judgments) (Scotland) Regulations 2005 (SSI 2005/629), reg 4. The 2005 Regulations, made under the power provided by s 219, partially replicate Art 3 of the Brussels IIa Regulation by providing that proceedings for the dissolution or annulment of a civil partnership may be brought in the Court of Session if both civil partners are habitually resident in Scotland; both civil partners were last habitually resident in Scotland and one of the civil partners continues to reside there; the defender is habitually resident in Scotland; the pursuer is habitually resident in Scotland and has resided there for at least 1 year immediately preceding the date on which the action is begun; or, the pursuer is domiciled and habitually resident in Scotland and has resided there for at least 6 months immediately preceding the date on which the action is begun. Proceedings for dissolution may also be brought in a sheriff court if the additional localising requirements of s 225(2) of the 2004 Act are satisfied.

If jurisdiction cannot be founded on one of the above grounds then s 225 provides two further bases on which the Court of Session will have jurisdiction. First, s 225(1)(b) grants jurisdiction on the ground that either civil partner is domiciled in Scotland on the date when the proceedings are begun. Again, an action may be brought on this ground in a sheriff court if additional requirements are fulfilled. Finally, s 225(1)(c) provides a ground of jurisdiction based not on a personal connection between the parties and Scotland, but on the fact that the partnership was registered in Scotland. This ground may be utilised only in the Court of Session when that court is satisfied that it is in the interests of justice to assume jurisdiction in the case. This final ground allows the Scottish courts to act as a *forum necessitatis* most obviously in circumstances where a civil partnership was previously registered in Scotland by parties one of whom now wishes to dissolve the relationship but lives in a country which does not permit such proceedings.

Although the primary grounds of jurisdiction are modelled on the Brussels IIa Regulation, such replication is not extended to the *lis pendens* rule of Art 19 and, instead, provision is made in s 226 and accompanying secondary legislation for the implementation of rules replicating the system of mandatory and discretionary sists found in Sch 3 to the Domicile and Matrimonial Proceedings Act 1973.

CHOICE OF LAW

At common law, when only the courts of the husband's domicile had jurisdiction, and the domicile of the wife would follow that of her husband, no choice of law issues arose as both the *lex fori* and the *lex domicilii* would be the same. The liberalisation of the grounds of jurisdiction introduced by the 1973 Act, accompanied by the abolition of the married woman's domicile, meant that such unity was no longer guaranteed. The possibility of a lack of unity between the forum and the domicile or nationality of the spouses has been further increased by the broad jurisdictional rules of Art 3 based principally on habitual residence. While many European countries have acknowledged choice of law issues in divorce by allowing for the application of a law other than that of the forum, usually the law of the parties' common nationality, the United Kingdom has rigidly adhered to the application of the *lex fori*. As a consequence, the United Kingdom decided not to opt into Council Regulation (EU) No 1259/2010 of 20 December 2010 implementing enhanced co-operation in the area of the law applicable to divorce and legal separation (commonly referred to as the "Rome III Regulation"). This Regulation sets out uniform rules of applicable law for divorce and legal separation in the 15 participating Member States based on a limited degree of party autonomy to choose the applicable law and, in the absence of choice, a cascade of alternatives.

RECOGNITION OF FOREIGN DECREES

Historically, a foreign decree of divorce would be recognised only if it were granted by a court of the husband's domicile. This strict rule was gradually loosened over time, with the decision in *Indyka* v *Indyka* (1969) greatly increasing the circumstances in which a foreign decree of divorce would be recognised. This was quickly followed by the Hague Convention of 1 June 1970 on the Recognition of Divorces and Legal Separations, implemented in the United Kingdom by the Recognition of Divorces and

Legal Separations Act 1971. The 1971 Act was repealed and replaced by the Family Law Act 1986, Pt II of which contains the relevant rules for the recognition of decrees granted both in the British Isles and overseas. This reference to "overseas" decrees must now be understood in light of the harmonised European rules of recognition found in the Brussels IIa Regulation which apply to judgments given in a Member State. Thus, the Regulation will apply to divorces granted in a Member State (excluding Denmark), while the 1986 Act continues to govern the recognition of "non-European" divorces, which includes divorces from elsewhere in the British Isles and from Denmark. Section 37 of the Family Law (Scotland) Act 2006 introduced amendments to the Domicile and Matrimonial Proceedings Act 1973 which permit the Court of Session and the sheriff court to grant declarator of recognition, or non-recognition, of a matrimonial decree granted outside the European Union.

Recognition under the Brussels IIa Regulation

Under the Regulation a judgment given in a Member State will be recognised in other Member States without any special procedure being required (Art 21(1)). A judgment is defined in Art 2(4) as one for divorce, legal separation or marriage annulment whatever the judgment may be called. There is no explicit requirement that the judgment must relate to an opposite-sex union, with the consequence that judgments relating to same-sex marriages would probably also come within the scope of the Regulation, at least in those Member States that permit such unions. Automatic recognition is subject to the fact that any interested party may apply for a decision that the judgment not be recognised (Art 21(3)). The grounds of non-recognition are limited to those found in Art 22 which relate to issues of public policy (Art 22(a)), natural justice (Art 22(b)) and irreconcilable judgments (Art 22(c) and (d)).

Under the first ground of Art 22(a), recognition will be refused if such recognition would be manifestly contrary to the public policy of the Member State in which recognition is sought. This is an exceptionally high standard to meet and recourse to this ground is further limited by the fact that the public policy exception may never be utilised in order to review the jurisdiction of the court of origin (Art 24). Consequently, a judgment must be recognised even if the court of origin assumed jurisdiction incorrectly. Further, Art 26 provides that under no circumstances may a judgment be reviewed as to its substance, and Art 25 makes clear that recognition may not be refused because the law of the Member State in which such recognition is sought would not allow divorce, legal separation or marriage annulment on the same facts.

The second ground relates to circumstances in which a judgment has been granted in default of appearance but will not be available when the respondent has accepted the judgment unequivocally (Art 22(b)). The third and fourth grounds relate to irreconcilable judgments (Art 22(c) and (d)). These judgments must have been given in proceedings involving the same parties but the cause of action need not be identical. The provisions extend to those judgments of non-Member States which are recognised in the Member State in which recognition is sought. Although the incidence of irreconcilable judgments emanating from different Member States will be limited by the strict system of *lis pendens* discussed earlier, since there is no possibility of staying proceedings where there is competing litigation outside of Europe, the existence of a conflicting non-European matrimonial decree is the most likely problem to occur in practice.

Recognition under the Family Law Act 1986

The 1986 Act distinguishes between those decrees obtained "by means of proceedings" and decrees obtained "otherwise than by means of proceedings". The 1986 Act contains no detailed guidance on the distinction between those two categories but the decision of the House of Lords in *Quazi* v *Quazi* (1980), interpreting similar wording in the Recognition of Divorces and Legal Separations Act 1971, shows that even relatively minimal formalities will be enough to constitute "proceedings" for the purposes of the 1986 Act. In contrast, in *Chaudhary* v *Chaudhary* (1985) the English Court of Appeal decided that the mere declaration of a husband that he wished to divorce his wife (an act that was effective to dissolve the marriage under the law in force in Kashmir), did not amount to "proceedings".

Divorces obtained by means of proceedings

Section 44(2) of the 1986 Act facilitates the automatic recognition throughout the British Islands, meaning the United Kingdom, the Channel Islands and the Isle of Man, of divorces, annulments and judicial separations granted therein. Such orders cannot be challenged on grounds of jurisdiction. Recognition may be refused in Scotland only on the ground of irreconcilability (s 51(1)) or if the order was granted or obtained at a time when, according to Scots law, there was no subsisting marriage between the parties (s 51(2)). This intra-UK scheme is restricted to orders granted by a court of civil jurisdiction (s 44(1)) and does not extend to extra-judicial proceedings.

The recognition of overseas divorces obtained by means of proceedings is governed by s 46(1) which provides that such divorces (and annulments and legal separations) will be recognised if effective under the law of the country in which it was obtained (s 46(1)(a)) and, at the date of the commencement of proceedings, at least one party to the marriage was habitually resident, domiciled in, or a national of that country (s 46(1)(b)). A party will be considered domiciled in a country if he was domiciled in that country according to either the law of that country in family matters or according to the law of the part of the United Kingdom in which the question of recognition arises (s 46(5)).

Recognition of an overseas divorce may be refused on the ground of irreconcilability (s 51(1)), or if the order was granted or obtained at a time when, according to Scots law, there was no subsisting marriage between the parties (s 51(2)). Recognition may also be refused in circumstances where there has been a lack of notice of the proceedings given to a party to the marriage (s 51(3)(a)(i)). It has been held in England that a foreign decree that is otherwise entitled to recognition under s 46 could be refused recognition under s 51(3)(a)(i) if at the time the foreign decree was obtained the spouses were living in England and reasonable steps, interpreted according to English law and concepts, were not taken to notify the other spouse to the foreign proceedings (*D* v *D* (*Recognition of Foreign Divorce*) (1994)). Recognition may also be refused if one of the parties had an inadequate opportunity to take part in the foreign proceedings (s 51(3)(a)(ii)). To avoid duplication with s 51(3)(a)(i), the reason for the lack of participation must be for something other than an absence of notice. Finally, recognition may be refused where such recognition would be manifestly contrary to public policy (s 51(3)(c)).

Section 50 of the 1986 Act provides that where an overseas divorce is recognised in any part of the United Kingdom under these provisions, the fact that it would not be recognised elsewhere does not preclude either party to the marriage from re-marrying in the United Kingdom, or cause the re-marriage of either party (wherever that may occur) to be treated as invalid in the United Kingdom. For example, a party will be able to marry in Scotland following the granting of an overseas divorce even if that divorce is not recognised under the law of his domicile. In other words, the rules of recognition discussed in this chapter take priority over the rules of capacity contained in s 38 of the Family Law (Scotland) Act 2006 and discussed in Chapter 7.

Divorces obtained otherwise than by means of proceedings

The recognition of overseas divorces (and annulments and legal separations) obtained otherwise than by means of proceedings is governed by s 46(2). This section mirrors s 46(1) in requiring that the divorce be effective under the law of the country in which it was obtained (s 46(2)) but is more onerous in that in also requires that, at the date on which the divorce was obtained, each party was domiciled in that country (s 46(2)(b)(i)) or either party to the marriage was domiciled in that country and the other party was domiciled in a country under whose law the divorce is recognised as valid (s 46(2)(b)(ii)). Further, even if these requirements are fulfilled, recognition will not be extended to such a divorce where either party to the marriage was habitually resident in the United Kingdom throughout the period of 1 year immediately preceding the date on which it was obtained (s 46(2)(c)). As with s 46(1), a party to a marriage will be treated as domiciled in a country if he was domiciled in that country either according to the law of that country in family matters or according to the law of the part of the United Kingdom in which the question of recognition arises.

As with divorces obtained by means of proceedings, recognition of an overseas divorce obtained otherwise than by means of proceedings may be refused on the ground of irreconcilability (s 51(1)), if it was granted at a time when, according to the law of Scotland, there was no subsisting marriage between the parties (s 51(2)), or when recognition would be manifestly contrary to public policy (s 51(3)(c)). An overseas divorce obtained otherwise than by means of proceedings may also be denied recognition in the absence of an official document certifying its effectiveness under the law of the country in which it was obtained (s 51(3)(b)(i)) or, in circumstances where the parties are not all domiciled in the country in which the divorce is obtained, in the absence of an official document certifying its recognition in the country of domicile (s 51(3)(b)(ii)).

Civil partnerships

The recognition of judgments concerning civil partnerships mirrors the scheme considered above in relation to marriage by distinguishing between domestic, European Union and overseas judgments. Judgments from elsewhere in the United Kingdom are governed by s 233 of the 2004 Act, with only minor differences to the equivalent provisions of the Family Law Act 1986. The recognition of EU judgments, which in this context includes Denmark, is governed by the Civil Partnership (Jurisdiction and Recognition of Judgments) (Scotland) Regulations 2005 (SSI 2005/629). These Regulations mostly mirror the equivalent terms of the Brussels IIa Regulation. Sections 234–238 provide for the recognition or non-recognition of overseas judgments by replicating the provisions of the Family Law Act 1986 discussed above.

Essential Facts

- A Scottish court will have jurisdiction to entertain an action for divorce or separation if it has jurisdiction under the Brussels IIa Regulation or if the action is an excluded action and either of the spouses is domiciled in Scotland on the date when the action is begun (Domicile and Matrimonial Proceedings Act 1973, s 7(2A)).
- If jurisdiction is taken under the Brussels IIa Regulation then *lis pendens* will apply to a conflict of jurisdiction; if jurisdiction is taken under the residual ground then the system of mandatory and discretionary sists provided by Sch 3 to the 1973 Act will be applicable.
- Jurisdiction to dissolve a civil partnership is governed by ss 219 and 225 of the Civil Partnership Act 2004 and the Civil Partnership (Jurisdiction and Recognition of Judgments) (Scotland) Regulations 2005 (SSI 2005/629), reg 4.
- A judgment given in one Member State will be recognised automatically in all other Member States, subject to the limited grounds of non-recognition contained in Art 22 of Brussels IIa.
- The recognition of judgments granted in a country outside the European Union is governed by the Family Law Act 1986 which distinguishes between divorces obtained by means of proceedings (s 46(1)) and divorces obtained otherwise than by means of proceedings (s 46(2)).

Essential Cases

Sundelind Lopez v Lopez Lizazo (2008): residual grounds of jurisdiction may be utilised only when the respondent spouse is not "European" in terms of Art 6 and no other court of a Member State has jurisdiction under the Brussels IIa Regulation (Art 7).

De Dampierre v De Dampierre (1988): a discretionary sist under Sch 3, para 9 to the 1973 Act is the statutory equivalent of the *forum non conveniens* doctrine.

Quazi v Quazi (1980): relatively minimal formalities will be enough to constitute "proceedings" for the purposes of the Family Law Act 1986.

9 THE PROPRIETARY CONSEQUENCES OF MARRIAGE AND DIVORCE

This chapter will consider the effect of marriage and divorce upon the property rights of the parties thereto. Although principally concerned with the law as applicable to marriage, brief consideration will be given at the end of the chapter to the proprietary consequences of other adult relationships, namely civil partnership and *de facto* cohabitation.

MARRIAGE

The effect that marriage has on property rights differs significantly from one legal system to another. Many jurisdictions adopt a system of matrimonial regimes under which a community of property exists, with the consequence that the marriage has the effect of vesting the property, owned by either spouse at the time of the marriage or acquired during its subsistence, in both spouses jointly. However, such matrimonial property regimes vary significantly in their scope, particularly as regards the precise property that will be included within the regime. Moreover, most matrimonial property regimes operate as the default system to be applied in the absence of choice, with parties permitted, to varying degrees, to exercise autonomy in coming to their own arrangements. In contrast, Scotland adopts a system of separation of property under which a marriage, subject to some exceptions, has no effect on the property rights of the spouses (Family Law (Scotland) Act 1985, s 24), with spouses being free to enter into an agreement to regulate their proprietary relations should they so wish (Family Law (Scotland) Act 2006, s 39(6)(b)).

Matrimonial regimes implied by statute

In many legal systems, particularly those of continental Europe, the absence of an express agreement between the spouses will result in the application of a default statutory regime establishing a community of property as between the spouses. In Scotland, the decision of the House of Lords in *Lashley* v *Hog* (1804) was previously thought to prevent such default foreign regimes being given effect. This decision was distinguished by the same court in the English case of *De Nicols* v *Curlier* (1900) on the basis that the question in *Lashley* was not one of matrimonial property at all but one referable to the law of succession. Consequently, the House of Lords in *De*

Nicols gave effect to a French system of community of goods which oper-
ated in the absence of express agreement.

The rights which spouses acquire under a default statutory regime are
thought to vest at the point of the marriage, even if the spouses subsequently become domiciled elsewhere. This is known as the doctrine of
immutability. Although the decision in *Lashley* could be interpreted as
applying the doctrine of mutability, whereby rights in matrimonial property would adapt to the changed circumstances of the spouses, this decision
can once again be distinguished on the basis that it is actually concerned
with the law of succession rather than the law relating to matrimonial
property regimes. Instead, the doctrine of immutability finds support in
De Nicols, in which two French citizens, domiciled in France, married in
that country in 1854 without entering into a written contract. The parties
subsequently relocated to England and became domiciled in that country.
When the husband died in 1897 it was held by the House of Lords that
the proprietary rights created by the original matrimonial regime persisted
and the wife therefore remained entitled to that property which fell within
the French system of community of goods applicable at the time of the
marriage.

Marriage contracts

In the absence of a default system of community of goods, or in place of
such a system should the system permit its own displacement, spouses may
enter into a private marriage contract to regulate their proprietary relations.
Such contracts are expressly excluded from the provisions of the Rome I
Regulation on the law applicable to contractual obligations (Art 1(2)(c)).
The consequence of this is that a marriage contract will be governed by the
rules of the common law in that the proper law of a marriage contract will
be considered to be either the law agreed by the parties, whether expressly
or by implication, or, failing such agreement, the law with which the
contract has the most real and substantial connection.

A marriage contract will be considered to be valid as to form if it complies
with the requirements of either the law of the place of execution or the
proper law. Essential validity is to be determined by the law with reference
to which the contract was made, and which was intended by the parties to
govern their rights and liabilities, namely the proper law. If the proper law
has not been chosen expressly, the courts will consider the circumstances
and terms of the contract to ascertain what intention should be imputed
to the parties. The most important factor in this determination will be the
domicile of the parties but other factors may also be relevant, depending on
the specific circumstances. The proper law will also apply equally to both

moveable and immoveable property, although its application to the latter will be subject to the *lex situs*.

The law applicable to issues of capacity is yet to be determined definitively, with the balance of English authority, and an analogy with the topic of commercial contracts, pointing towards the proper law of the contract. However, the decision of the House of Lords in *Cooper* v *Cooper* (1888), on appeal from Scotland, has been interpreted as pointing towards the applicable law as being the domiciliary law of the person whose capacity is at issue, especially where this coincides with the *lex loci contractus*. Revocability is an issue for the proper law of the contract, while capacity to revoke is an issue for the law of the domicile of the party at the time of the revocation (*Sawrey-Cookson* v *Sawrey-Cookson's Trustees* (1905)). As regards immoveables, capacity will be referred to the *lex situs* of the property (*Black* v *Black's Trustees* (1950)).

No implied regime or marriage contract

In the absence of both an implied default statutory scheme and a bespoke marriage contract, reference must be made to s 39 of the Family Law (Scotland) Act 2006 in order to identify the applicable law. Section 39(1) states that any question in relation to the rights of spouses to each other's immoveable property arising by virtue of the marriage shall be determined by the law of the place in which the property is situated. Section 39(4) extends the application of the *lex situs* to the use or occupation of a matrimonial home which is moveable and the use of the contents of a matrimonial home (whether the home is moveable or immoveable). Where the spouses are domiciled in the same country, any question in relation to the rights of the spouses to each other's moveable property shall be determined by the law of that country (s 39(2)). If the spouses are domiciled in different countries they shall be taken to have the same rights to such property as they had immediately before the marriage (s 39(3)). Should a spouse change his or her domicile this will not affect a vested right in moveable property which existed immediately before the change (s 39(5)). These rules do not apply in relation to the law on aliment, financial provision on divorce, or to the transfer of property on divorce or succession (s 39(6)(a)).

DIVORCE

A Scottish court will have jurisdiction to make orders for financial provision if it has jurisdiction to make a decree of divorce, separation or nullity of marriage (Domicile and Matrimonial Proceedings Act 1973, s 10(1)). Accordingly, where a Scottish court has jurisdiction either under Art 3 of the Brussels IIa Regulation or via the residual rule contained in s 7(2A)(b) of the 1973 Act it will also have jurisdiction over the financial aspects of divorce. Upon assuming such jurisdiction, the ownership of marital property will be determined according to the provisions of the Family Law (Scotland) Act 1985. Stated succinctly, the 1985 Act defines matrimonial property as all property belonging to the parties (s 10(4)) at the date on which the parties cease to cohabit (s 10(3)). This property must have been acquired during the marriage, otherwise than by way of gift or succession, though, in the case of property intended for use as a family home or as furniture or plenishings for such a home, it may be acquired before the date of marriage (s 10(4)). The net value of the matrimonial property will be shared fairly between the parties, with fairness equated to equal sharing unless such other proportions are justified by special circumstances (s 10(1)).

Part IV of the Matrimonial and Family Proceedings Act 1984 furnishes the Scottish courts with the jurisdiction to make orders for financial provision following a foreign divorce. This power will be available only when the strict jurisdictional requirements and additional conditions of s 28 are satisfied. Section 28 requires both parties to have a connection to Scotland. For the applicant, this connection must be in the form of domicile or habitual residence on the date the application is made (s 28(2)(a)). The other party to the marriage must also have a connection to Scotland and this may be in terms of domicile or habitual residence either on the date the application is made (s 28(2)(b)(i)) or at the time when the parties last lived together as husband and wife (s 28(2)(b)(ii)). A connection can also be established via the ownership of property if, on the date when the application is made, the other party was an owner or tenant of, or had a beneficial interest in, property in Scotland which had at some time been a matrimonial home of the parties (s 28(2)(b)(iii)). If an application is made on this final jurisdictional ground then the court is limited in the orders it may make to an order relating to that former matrimonial home or its furniture and plenishings, or an order that the other party to the marriage shall pay to the applicant a capital sum not exceeding the value of that other party's interest in the former matrimonial home and its furniture and plenishings (s 29(5)). Further localisation requirements apply when the action is brought in a sheriff court (s 28(2)(c)).

Section 28(3) details a further six conditions that must be met before the court may entertain an application by one of the parties for an order for financial provision. If both the jurisdictional requirements of s 28(2) and the additional conditions of s 28(3) are satisfied, the application for an order for financial provision will be governed by Scots law as it would apply if the application were being made in an action for divorce in Scotland (s 29). In relevant cases, the provisions of Pt IV will be superseded by the terms of Council Regulation (EC) No 4/2009 of 18 December 2008 on jurisdiction, applicable law, recognition and enforcement of decisions and co-operation in matters relating to maintenance obligations.

CIVIL PARTNERSHIP

Following the underlying principle of the Civil Partnership Act 2004, civil partners are treated identically to spouses as regards matrimonial property and financial provision following the dissolution of a civil partnership. Consequently, the terms of the 2004 Act and the amendments introduced thereby ensure that what is said above in relation to spouses can be applied to civil partners *mutatis mutandis*.

COHABITATION

Sections 25–30 of the Family Law (Scotland) Act 2006 provide cohabitants, as defined in s 25, with limited proprietary and financial rights. Outwith the jurisdictional criteria applicable in respect of an action by a surviving cohabitation for provision on intestacy (s 29), the provisions of the 2006 Act are silent as to their private international law implications. In *Kerr* v *Mangan* 2014 CSIH 69, 2014 SLT 866 the Inner House of the Court of Session held that s29 only applied to land situated in Scotland and did not apply to land situated elsewhere.

Essential Facts

- Scotland adopts a system of separation of property under which a marriage, subject to some exceptions, has no effect on the property rights of the spouses (Family Law (Scotland) Act 1985, s 24). In contrast, many other countries enforce matrimonial property regimes which create a community of property as between the spouses.
- The rights which spouses acquire under a default statutory regime are thought to vest at the point of the marriage, even if the spouses subsequently become domiciled elsewhere. This is known as the doctrine of immutability.
- The proper law of a marriage contract is the law chosen by the parties or, in the absence of such agreement, the law with which the contract has the most real and substantial connection.

- Section 39 of the Family Law (Scotland) Act 2006 identifies the law applicable to determine matrimonial property rights in the absence of both an implied statutory scheme and a marriage contract.
- A Scottish court will have jurisdiction to make orders for financial provision if it has jurisdiction to make a decree of divorce, separation or nullity of marriage (Domicile and Matrimonial Proceedings Act 1973, s 10(1)). If jurisdiction exists, the ownership of marital property will be determined according to the provisions of the Family Law (Scotland) Act 1985.
- Part IV of the Matrimonial and Family Proceedings Act 1984 furnishes the Scottish courts with the jurisdiction to make orders for financial provision following a foreign divorce. This power will be available only when the strict jurisdictional requirements and additional conditions of s 28 are satisfied.

10 MAINTENANCE

The principal legislative framework applicable to issues of maintenance is found in Council Regulation (EC) No 4/2009 of 18 December 2008 on jurisdiction, applicable law, recognition and enforcement of decisions and co-operation in matters relating to maintenance obligations (commonly referred to as the "Maintenance Regulation"), which came into force on 18 June 2011. The Maintenance Regulation applies to all maintenance obligations arising from a family relationship, parentage, marriage or affinity, with the term "maintenance obligation" to be given an autonomous interpretation (Recital (11) and Art 1). Matters relating to maintenance previously fell within the scope of the Brussels I Regulation and its predecessor the 1968 Brussels Convention but the Maintenance Regulation replaces these provisions and, accordingly, maintenance obligations are excluded specifically from the scope of the Brussels I Regulation (recast) in Art 1(2)(a). The Regulation applies in all Member States but, in relation to Denmark, only insofar as it amends the Brussels I Regulation.

JURISDICTION

Chapter II of the Maintenance Regulation details the jurisdictional rules applicable to matters relating to maintenance obligations. These rules bear a resemblance to those found in the Brussels I Regulation but have been refined in order to reflect the peculiarities of maintenance obligations. The general provisions as to jurisdiction are to be found in Art 3 which provides four alternative grounds of jurisdiction. First, jurisdiction will lie with the court for the place where the defendant is habitually resident (Art 3(a)), or the court for the place where the creditor is habitually resident (Art 3(b)). Article 3(c) provides that jurisdiction shall also lie with the court which, according to its own law, has jurisdiction to entertain proceedings concerning the status of a person if the matter relating to maintenance is ancillary to those proceedings, unless that jurisdiction is based solely on the nationality of one of the parties. A rule identical in its wording to Art 3(c) is contained in Art 3(d) regarding maintenance which is ancillary to parental responsibility proceedings. In the context of the United Kingdom and Ireland, the reference to "nationality" is to be read as a reference to domicile (Art 2(3)).

Article 4 adopts the principle of party autonomy by allowing parties to come to an agreement conferring jurisdiction on a court or the courts of a Member State to settle any disputes in matters relating to a maintenance obligation which have arisen or may arise between them. This agreement shall be in writing with any communication by electronic means which provides a durable record of the agreement being equivalent to writing (Art 4(2)). Party autonomy is limited, however, to those courts identified in Art 4(1), namely: the courts of the Member State in which one of the parties is habitually resident (Art 4(1)(a)); the courts of the Member State of which one of the parties has the nationality (or domicile in the case of the United Kingdom and Ireland) (Art 4(1)(b)); or, in the case of maintenance obligations between spouses or former spouses, the court which has jurisdiction to settle their dispute in matrimonial matters (Art 4(1)(c)(i)) or the courts of the Member State of the spouses' last common habitual residence where that endured for at least 1 year (Art 4(1)(c)(ii)). In each circumstance the condition stated has to be met at either the time the choice of court agreement is concluded or at the time the court is seised. An agreement coming within the scope of Art 4 will be treated as exclusive unless the parties have agreed otherwise. Party autonomy is also subject to a more general restriction in that Art 4 does not apply to a dispute relating to a maintenance obligation towards a child under the age of 18 (Art 4(3)). Jurisdiction will also exist in the court of a Member State before which the defendant enters an appearance other than to contest jurisdiction (Art 5).

Article 6 provides a ground of subsidiary jurisdiction available in circumstances where no Member State has jurisdiction under Arts 3, 4 or 5 and no state party to the 2007 Lugano Convention has jurisdiction under that instrument, the provisions of which remain applicable as regards the EFTA states. In such circumstances jurisdiction will lie with the courts of the Member State of the common nationality (or domicile in the case of the United Kingdom and Ireland) of the parties. For the purposes of Art 6, parties who have their domicile in different territorial units of the same Member State are treated as having their common domicile within that State (Art 2(3)). Finally, where no court of a Member State has jurisdiction pursuant to Arts 3, 4, 5 or 6, Art 7 provides that a Member State court which has "sufficient connection" with the dispute may, on an exceptional basis, hear the case if proceedings cannot reasonably be brought, or conducted, or would be impossible, in a third State with which the dispute is closely connected. Guidance on this article is found in Recital (16) which explains that a "sufficient connection" could be the nationality (or domicile) of just one of the parties and the "exceptional basis" justifying the use of this ground of jurisdiction may be deemed to exist when proceedings prove impossible in the third state of close connection because of civil war.

Article 8 seeks to prevent a maintenance debtor from modifying an existing order or bringing fresh proceedings in another Member State after a decision has been delivered. It applies both to judgments rendered in a Member State and also to judgments rendered in a Contracting State to the Hague Convention of 23 November 2007 on the International Recovery of Child Support and Other Forms of Family Maintenance. Subject to the exceptions listed in Art 8(2), Art 8(1) provides a negative rule of jurisdiction in stating that, where a decision is given in either a Member or Contracting State in which the creditor is habitually resident, proceedings to modify the decision or to have a new decision given cannot be brought by the debtor in any other Member State as long as the creditor remains habitually resident in the state of origin.

Articles 9–14 contain provisions replicating those found in the Brussels I Regulation in providing an autonomous definition of the time at which the court will be deemed to be seised (Art 9), implementing the *lis pendens* system of jurisdiction allocation (Art 12) and delimiting the approach of the courts when related actions are pending in the courts of different Member States (Art 13). Article 10 requires that a court of a Member State seised of a case over which it has no jurisdiction shall declare of its own motion that it has no jurisdiction. Article 11 provides special rules as to the service of process when the defendant is habitually resident in a state other than the Member State where the action is brought and does not enter an appearance. Article 14 governs provisional and protective measures.

CHOICE OF LAW

Chapter III of the Maintenance Regulation contains a single article, Art 15, which does not provide explicit choice of law rules but instead states that the law applicable to maintenance obligations shall be determined in accordance with the Hague Protocol of 23 November 2007 on the Law Applicable to Maintenance Obligations in the Member States bound by that instrument. The 2007 Hague Protocol provides a general rule that maintenance obligations shall be governed by the law of the state of the habitual residence of the creditor, save where the Protocol provides otherwise (Art 3). The United Kingdom declined to opt into the decision of the European Union to sign and ratify the 2007 Hague Protocol and is therefore not bound by its terms. Accordingly, s 40 of the Family Law (Scotland) Act 2006 provides that a Scottish court will apply Scots internal law in any action for aliment which comes before it, subject to the limited exceptions found in the Maintenance Orders (Reciprocal Enforcement) Act 1972.

RECOGNITION AND ENFORCEMENT

Chapter IV of the Maintenance Regulation contains provisions as to the recognition and enforcement of maintenance decisions, with different rules applying depending on the Member State from which the decision emanates. This distinction has been drawn on the basis of whether the Member State of origin is bound by the 2007 Hague Protocol (Art 16). Articles 17–22 apply to those states that are so bound, Arts 23–38 to those that are not. Articles 39–43 apply regardless of the Member State of origin. The United Kingdom and Denmark are the only Member States not to be bound by the 2007 Hague Protocol.

Decisions given in a Member State bound by the 2007 Hague Protocol

Article 17 abolishes *exequatur* in requiring that a decision given in a Member State will be recognised in another Member State without any special procedure being required and without any possibility of opposing its recognition (Art 17(1)). Such a decision will also be enforced in another Member State without the need for a declaration of enforceability (Art 17(2)). Procedural fairness for defendants who did not enter an appearance in the Member State of origin is provided by the review mechanism of Art 19. The review must occur in the Member State of origin and only in the circumstances detailed in the article. The opportunity for the defendant to utilise this review procedure is subject to a time limit specified in Art 19(2). If the court of origin accepts the application for review, the maintenance decision shall be null and void. If, however, the court rejects the application then the decision will remain in force (Art 19(3)). The decision will be enforced in another Member State upon production of the relevant documents specified in Art 20. Article 21 details the limited grounds on which enforcement may be refused or suspended. First, enforcement may be refused if the right to enforce is extinguished by the effect of prescription or the limitation of action, under the law of either the Member State of origin or the Member State of enforcement – whichever provides for the longer limitation period (Art 21(2)). Second, enforcement may also be refused if the original decision is irreconcilable with a decision given in the Member State of enforcement or with a decision given in another Member State or in a third state which fulfils the conditions necessary for its recognition in the Member State of enforcement (Art 21(2)). Finally, enforcement *may* be suspended where the court of the Member State of origin has been seised of an Art 19 review application and *shall* be suspended where the enforceability of the decision is suspended in the Member State of origin (Art 21(3)).

Decisions given in a Member State not bound by the 2007 Hague Protocol

The procedures for the recognition and enforcement of decisions given in a Member State not bound by the 2007 Hague Protocol (which, from the viewpoint of the United Kingdom, relate only to Denmark) are modelled on the equivalent provisions contained in the Brussels I Regulation (Recital (26)). The key difference in comparison with those decisions given in Member States that are bound by the 2007 Hague Protocol is to be found in the fact that a decision from the United Kingdom or Denmark will be enforceable only in another Member State when it has been declared enforceable there (Art 26). The application for a declaration of enforceability, referred to in the United Kingdom as a "registration for enforcement", must be accompanied by specific documentation as detailed in Art 28. Article 24 identifies the grounds on which recognition may be refused and these mirror Art 34 of the Brussels I Regulation in referring to public policy, natural justice and irreconcilability.

Assuming compliance with the required formalities, a decision will be declared enforceable without any review and without the party against whom enforcement is sought being able to make any submissions (Art 30). Thereafter both parties will be notified (Art 31) and an appeal can be lodged in accordance with the procedures in Art 32. The court with which the appeal is lodged shall revoke a registration only on those grounds specified in Art 24.

United Kingdom orders

The free movement of orders for aliment or maintenance between the territorial units of the United Kingdom is governed by the Maintenance Orders Act 1950, s 17(2) of which provides that an order made in one part of the United Kingdom may be registered in the court of another part if the person liable to make the payments resides in that other part and it is convenient that the order should be enforceable there. The discretion exercisable under this section lies with the court of origin, not the court of registration. An order so registered in another part of the United Kingdom may be enforced in that part of the United Kingdom as if it had been made by the registering court (s 18(1)).

Other regimes

A variety of other instruments and agreements play a role in facilitating the recognition and enforcement of maintenance orders, the applicability of which depends on the identity of the country from which the order originates. For example, Pt I of the Maintenance Orders (Reciprocal

Enforcement) Act 1972 provides a system of reciprocal enforcement operative between the United Kingdom and reciprocating Commonwealth countries.

Essential Facts

- This area is governed primarily by Council Regulation (EC) No 4/2009 of 18 December 2008 on jurisdiction, applicable law, recognition and enforcement of decisions and co-operation in matters relating to maintenance obligations (commonly referred to as the "Maintenance Regulation").
- Chapter II of the Regulation details the jurisdictional rules applicable to matters relating to maintenance obligations.
- Parties may agree that a particular court or courts of a Member State shall have jurisdiction to settle any disputes in matters relating to maintenance obligations but this choice is limited to those courts identified in Art 4.
- Section 40 of the Family Law (Scotland) Act 2006 provides that a Scottish court will apply Scots internal law in any action for aliment which comes before it, subject to the limited exceptions found in the Maintenance Orders (Reciprocal Enforcement) Act 1972.
- The Regulation applies different rules regarding the recognition and enforcement of maintenance decisions depending on whether or not the Member State of origin is bound by the Hague Protocol of 23 November 2007 on the Law Applicable to Maintenance Obligations.
- For those Member States bound by the 2007 Hague Protocol, *exequatur* has been abolished and a decision given in such a Member State will be recognised and enforced in all other Member States without any special procedure being required (Art 17).
- A decision from a Member State not bound by the 2007 Hague Protocol (the United Kingdom and Denmark) shall be enforceable in another Member State when it has been declared enforceable there (Art 26).

11 CHILDREN

Questions of private international law in relation to children arise in a number of different contexts. This chapter will consider the private international law issues relevant to children with regard to matters of status, parental responsibility, abduction and adoption. The importance of the latter three areas continues to rise as a consequence of the growth in international mobility leading to an increase in families with links to more than one jurisdiction.

STATUS

In Scotland the concepts of legitimacy and illegitimacy, and the differences premised upon this categorisation, were abolished by the Family Law (Scotland) Act 2006. Section 21(2)(a) of the 2006 Act, which introduced a new s 1(1) to the Law Reform (Parent and Child) (Scotland) Act 1986, provides that no person whose status is governed by Scots law shall be illegitimate and, accordingly, the fact that a person's parents are not or have not been married to each other shall be left out of account in determining the person's legal status or establishing the legal relationship between the person and any other person.

As this amendment only applies to a person "whose status is governed by Scots law", the marital status of a person's parents may still be a relevant consideration for those persons whose status is not governed by Scots law, most notably when a Scottish court may be required to apply a foreign law in matters related to succession. Previously, problems of circularity bedevilled this area as under the common law the determination of domicile depended on legitimacy but the status of legitimacy was to be determined by a person's domicile. The 2006 Act has removed this problem in providing statutory rules for both the determination of status and the identification of domicile. Thus, s 41 of the 2006 Act provides that any question as to the effect on a person's status of the fact that the person's parents are, or have been, married to each other (or, are not married to each other) will be determined by the law of the country in which the person is domiciled at the time at which the question arises. Domicile will be determined in accordance with s 22, under which no reference is made to the marital status of the parents.

PARENTAL RESPONSIBILITY

Jurisdiction

There are three distinct jurisdictional regimes relating to matters of parental responsibility: Council Regulation (EC) No 2201/2003 of 27 November 2003 concerning jurisdiction and the recognition and enforcement of judgments in matrimonial matters and the matters of parental responsibility, repealing Regulation (EC) No 1347/2000 (commonly referred to as the "Brussels IIa Regulation"); the Hague Convention of 19 October 1996 on Jurisdiction, Applicable Law, Recognition, Enforcement and Co-operation in Respect of Parental Responsibility and Measures for the Protection of Children; and the rules of the Family Law Act 1986. There is a clear hierarchy between these regimes, with the Brussels IIa Regulation at the apex and the rules of the 1996 Hague Convention and the 1986 Act subordinate thereto.

The Brussels IIa Regulation

The Brussels IIa Regulation provides uniform jurisdictional rules in civil matters for the attribution, exercise, delegation, restriction or termination of parental responsibility (Art 1(1)(b)). The Regulation applies throughout the European Union with the exclusion of Denmark. The phrase "civil matters" is to be given an autonomous meaning and may therefore extend to measures which would be considered to be a matter of public law within the domestic legal system of a Member State (*Proceedings Brought by A* (2010)). Article 1(2) identifies a number of matters to which the Regulation will apply while Art 1(3) lists those matters which fall outside the scope of the Regulation. "Parental responsibility" is further defined in Art 2(7) as referring to all rights and duties relating to the person or the property of a child which are given to a natural or legal person by judgment, by operation of law or by an agreement having legal effect, including rights of custody and rights of access.

Article 8 (general jurisdiction): Article 8 establishes the primary jurisdictional rule in matters of parental responsibility in that jurisdiction will lie with the courts of the Member State in which the child is habitually resident at the time the court is seised in terms of Art 16. A child will be habitually resident in a Member State in which he is physically present, with this presence not in any way temporary or intermittent but reflecting some degree of integration in a social and family environment. Factors relevant in the identification of habitual residence include, but are not limited to, the duration, regularity, conditions and reasons for the stay in a Member State and the family's move to that state, the child's nationality, the place and conditions of attendance at school, linguistic knowledge, and the family and social relationships of the child in that state (*Proceedings Brought by A* (2010)). This ground of jurisdiction is subject to the provisions of Arts 9, 10 (discussed below) and 12 which deal with issues of continuing jurisdiction, jurisdiction in cases of child abduction and prorogation of jurisdiction respectively.

Article 9 (continuing jurisdiction): Once the court of a Member State is seised under Art 8 it may continue to have jurisdiction under Art 9 even after a change in the child's habitual residence, thus preventing the courts in the Member State of the child's new habitual residence taking jurisdiction under Art 8. This right of continuing jurisdiction applies only to access rights; it does not extend to other matters of parental responsibility. For the continuing jurisdiction of Art 9 to be effective the court originally seised under Art 8 must have issued a judgment on access rights before the child lawfully acquired a new habitual residence in another Member State while the holder of the access rights must continue to have his habitual residence in the Member State of the child's former habitual residence (Art 9(1)). If these requirements are satisfied then the court originally seised under Art 8 will retain jurisdiction during a three-month period following the move for the purpose of modifying a judgment on access rights previously issued (Art 9(1)). This continuing jurisdiction will not apply if the holder of access rights has accepted the jurisdiction of the courts of the Member State of the child's new habitual residence by participating in proceedings before those courts without contesting jurisdiction (Art 9(2)). Moreover, the provisions of Art 9 do not prevent the courts of the Member State of the child's new habitual residence from exercising their Art 8 jurisdiction to decide matters of parental responsibility other than those relating to access rights.

Article 12 (prorogation of jurisdiction): Article 12 provides a limited measure of party autonomy in two distinct circumstances. First, Art 12(1) provides that a court of a Member State exercising jurisdiction in matrimonial proceedings under Art 3 will also have jurisdiction in matters relating to parental responsibility when at least one of the spouses has parental responsibility in relation to the child (Art 12(1)(a)) and the jurisdiction of the court has been accepted, expressly or otherwise in an unequivocal manner, by the spouses as well as any holders of parental responsibility (Art 12(1)(b)). Mere submission in matrimonial proceedings is not sufficient to indicate unequivocal acceptance of the jurisdiction of that same court in matters of parental responsibility (*Bush* v *Bush* (2008)). In addition, it must be in the "superior interests" of the child, a concept considered to be equivalent to the more familiar concept of the "best interests" of the child (*Re I (A Child) (Contact Application: Jurisdiction)* (2009)) for that court to take jurisdiction (Art 12(1)(b)). The jurisdiction conferred under Art 12(1) will cease upon the occurrence of one of the events listed in Art 12(2).

Alternatively, proceedings may also be brought under Art 12(3) in a Member State with which the child has a substantial connection and it is in his best interests for the proceedings to be brought in that state. This provision will be effective only when the jurisdiction of the courts has been accepted expressly or otherwise in an unequivocal manner by all the parties to the proceedings (Art 12(3)(b)). What may constitute a "substantial connection" includes, but is not limited to, the fact that one of the holders of parental responsibility is habitually resident in that Member State or that the child is a national of that Member State (Art 12(3)(a)).

Article 12(4) provides that, where a child has his habitual residence in the territory of a third state which is not a contracting party to the 1996 Hague Convention then jurisdiction under either Art 12(1) or (3) will be considered to be in the child's superior/best interests. This will be particularly so if it is impossible to hold proceedings in the third state in question.

Article 13 (presence): Should it not be possible to determine the habitual residence of the child, therefore precluding the application of Art 8, then, in the absence of an agreement under either limb of Art 12, proceedings may be brought on the basis of the child's presence in a Member State.

Article 14 (residual jurisdiction): Where no court of a Member State has jurisdiction pursuant to Arts 8–13, jurisdiction shall be determined, in each Member State, by the laws of that state. Any subsequent judgment will be recognised and enforced in other Member States pursuant to the rules of the Regulation. In Scotland this means that the Family Law Act 1986 retains a limited jurisdictional role, discussed further below.

Article 15 (transfer of jurisdiction): Article 15 constitutes a notable exception to the otherwise rigid system of the allocation of jurisdiction found within the Brussels family of instruments by permitting the transfer of jurisdiction to a court considered better placed to hear a case. This mechanism may operate regardless of the ground on which the original court takes jurisdiction but is only effective to transfer jurisdiction to the courts of another Member State.

Article 15(1) provides that a Member State court with jurisdiction which considers that the courts of another Member State with which the child has a particular connection, defined in Art 15(3), would be better placed to hear the case, may, if it is in the best interests of the child, request that the other Member State assume jurisdiction. The provision may be invoked by a party alone, by the court seised of its own motion, or, by a court in a Member State with which the child has one of the identified particular connections (Art 15(2)). Article 15(4)–(6) provides further detail as to the manner in which this power may be exercised.

Article 19 (*lis pendens*): The allocation of jurisdiction in a case of concurrent proceedings relating to parental responsibility will be determined according to the *lis pendens* rule considered in earlier chapters. Thus, where proceedings relating to parental responsibility relating to the same child and involving the same cause of action are brought before courts of different Member States, the court second seised shall of its own motion stay its proceedings until such time as the jurisdiction of the court first seised is established (Art 19(2)), at which point the court second seised shall decline jurisdiction in favour of that court (Art 19(3)), unless the court first seised stays its proceedings under Art 15.

Article 20 (provisional and protective measures): Article 20(1) of the Regulation provides that, in urgent cases, its provisions do not prevent the courts of a Member State from taking such provisional, including protective, measures in respect of persons or assets in that state as may be available under the law of that Member State, even if, under the Regulation, the court of another Member State has jurisdiction as to the substance of the matter. As an exception to the Regulation's system of jurisdiction, this basis must be interpreted strictly and relied on only in exceptional circumstances, such as where measures are necessary in a Member State other than that of the child's habitual residence in order to address a situation likely seriously to endanger the welfare of the child.

The 1996 Hague Convention

The 1996 Hague Convention came into force in the United Kingdom on 1 November 2012 and contains rules of jurisdiction which are similar, although not identical, to those contained in the Brussels IIa Regulation. The Convention defines "parental responsibility" as including parental authority, or any analogous relationship of authority determining the rights, powers and responsibilities of parents, guardians or other legal representatives in relation to the person or the property of the child (Art 1(2)) with Arts 3 and 4 setting out respectively what matters the Convention will, and will not, apply to. The sum of these provisions is that the material scope of the Convention equates to that of the Regulation.

Article 5 of the Convention gives jurisdiction to the state of the child's habitual residence, a rule which mirrors the general ground of jurisdiction under Art 8 of the Regulation. There is, however, no equivalent to the provision of Art 9 of the Regulation regarding continuing jurisdiction with regard to access rights following a change in the child's habitual residence. Instead, Art 5(2) of the Convention expressly states that, subject to Art 7, which is applicable in the context of child abduction, following a change of the child's habitual residence to another Contracting State, the authorities of the state of the new habitual residence will have jurisdiction. It is also possible for jurisdiction to be founded on the presence of the child in a Contracting State when habitual residence cannot be established (Art 6).

Article 10 of the Convention grants a limited right of prorogation – a right which is even more constrained that that available under the Regulation, as it allows only for the possibility of jurisdiction being taken by the matrimonial forum. Due to the global nature of the Convention, there is no requirement that the matrimonial forum be exercising jurisdiction by virtue of Art 3 of the Regulation. There is no equivalent of Art 12(3) of the Regulation which provides for jurisdiction being taken by the courts of a Member State with which the child has a substantial connection.

The transfer mechanism of Art 8, which inspired Art 15 of the Regulation, permits a case to be transferred to a Contracting State other than that state with jurisdiction under Arts 5 or 6 if that other state comes within the terms of Art 8(2). Article 8(2) is similar in its terms to Art 15(3) of the Regulation, which exhaustively defines those Member States which are considered to have a "particular connection" to the child but, importantly, Art 8(2) merely identifies, among other states, a state with which the child has a "substantial connection" – a term which is left undefined. Accordingly, the Convention potentially offers a wider choice of states to which proceedings may be transferred than that available under the Regulation. As in the Regulation, such a transfer of jurisdiction can be instigated by the authorities of a Contracting State to which jurisdiction could be transferred (Art 9).

The Convention also includes the possibility for temporary measures to be taken in cases of urgency (Art 11) or for the protection of the person or property of the child (Art 12). Article 13 contains a *lis pendens* clause but this is not applied as strictly as under the Regulation, notably as the court first seised is permitted to decline jurisdiction (Art 13(2)). In contrast with Art 14 of the Regulation, there is no rule in the Convention restricting the exercise of residual jurisdiction, with the consequence that recognition of a judgment may be refused under the Convention if jurisdiction was founded on a non-Convention ground (Art 23(2)(a)).

The respective spheres of operation of the 1996 Hague Convention and the Brussels IIa Regulation depend on the habitual residence of the child. If the child is habitually resident in an EU Member State, the Regulation will apply; if the child is habitually resident in a non-EU Contracting State, the Convention will apply (Convention, Art 52; Regulation, Art 61).

The Family Law Act 1986

Prior to the coming into force of the Brussels IIa Regulation and the 1996 Hague Convention, the jurisdiction of the Scottish courts to make an order with respect to the residence, custody, care or control of a child, contact with or access to a child, or the education or upbringing of a child was governed by Ch III of the Family Law Act 1986. These rules must now be read in light of s 17A of the 1986 Act (as introduced and subsequently amended by the European Communities (Matrimonial and Parental Responsibility Jurisdiction and Judgments) (Scotland) Regulations 2005 (SSI 2005/42) and the Parental Responsibility and Measures for the Protection of Children (International Obligations) (Scotland) Regulations 2010 (SSI 2010/213) respectively) which provides that the provisions of Ch III are "subject to Sections 2 and 3 of Chapter II of the Council Regulation and are subject to the Hague Convention". Consequently, recourse may be had to the provisions of the 1986 Act only when neither the Regulation nor the Convention is engaged.

Choice of law

While the Brussels IIa Regulation is limited to matters of jurisdiction and recognition and enforcement, the 1996 Hague Convention is broader in its scope by also identifying the law to be applied when jurisdiction is exercised thereunder. By virtue of r 6 of the Parental Responsibility and Measures for the Protection of Children (International Obligations) (Scotland) Regulations 2010 (SSI 2010/213) these choice of law provisions will also apply when jurisdiction is taken under the Regulation. However, the practical consequences of these choice of law provisions will be minimal as Art 15 of the Convention provides that, in exercising jurisdiction, the authorities of the Contracting States shall apply their own law. Accordingly, whenever a Scottish court takes jurisdiction under either the Regulation or the Convention, it will apply Scots law. Only in exceptional circumstances, insofar as the protection of the person or the property of the child requires, may the law of another state with which the situation has a substantial connection be applied or taken into consideration (Art 15(2)).

The attribution or extinction of parental responsibility by operation of law, without the intervention of a judicial or administrative authority, is governed by the law of the state of the habitual residence of the child (Art 16(1)). The attribution or extinction of parental responsibility by an agreement or a unilateral act, without intervention of a judicial or administrative authority, is governed by the law of the state of the child's habitual residence at the time when the agreement or unilateral act takes effect (Art 16(2)). A change in the child's habitual residence does not affect parental responsibility which exists under the law of the state of the previous habitual residence (Art 16(3)) but the attribution of parental responsibility by operation of law to a person who does not already have such responsibility is governed by the law of the state of the new habitual residence. The Convention thus promotes both the retention and the acquisition of parental responsibility. The exercise of parental responsibility is governed by the law of the state of the child's habitual residence. If the child's habitual residence changes, it is governed by the law of the State of the new habitual residence (Art 17).

Recognition and enforcement

The Brussels IIa Regulation

As with matrimonial matters, the mutual recognition of judgments relating to matters of parental responsibility is central to the operation of the Brussels IIa Regulation, with Art 21(1) providing that a judgment given in a Member State shall be recognised in all other Member States (excluding Denmark) without any special procedure being required. However, any interested party may apply for a decision that the judgment be or not be recognised (Art 21(3)) with the grounds of non-recognition being listed in Art 23. These grounds largely replicate those applicable to matrimonial judgments under Art 22, although they have been adapted and expanded in order to reflect specific issues relevant to judgments relating to parental responsibility. Further, the jurisdiction of the court of the Member State of origin may not be reviewed (Art 24), nor may a judgment be reviewed as to its substance (Art 26). With regard to enforcement, a judgment on the exercise of parental responsibility in respect of a child given in a Member State which is enforceable in that Member State and has been served shall be enforced in Scotland (or any other part of the United Kingdom) once it has been registered for enforcement (Art 28). The grounds for refusal of enforcement are the same as for the refusal of recognition.

The Regulation provides special rules relating to certain judgments concerning rights of access and of certain judgments which require the return of an abducted child given pursuant to Art 11(8) (Art 40). Such judgments given in one Member State will be recognised and enforced in other Member States automatically if the requirements of Ch III, s 4 of the Regulation are satisfied.

The 1996 Hague Convention

Similar, although not identical, provisions concerning recognition and enforcement are found in Ch IV of the 1996 Hague Convention. These provisions are distinguishable from their Brussels counterparts as they permit a greater degree of flexibility and judicial discretion than that found under the Brussels IIa Regulation. The Convention contains no equivalent to Ch III, s 4 of the Regulation regarding rights of access and return orders.

The Family Law Act 1986

Section 26(1) of the 1986 Act provides that an order relating to parental responsibilities or parental rights in relation to a child which is made outside the United Kingdom shall be recognised in Scotland if the order was made in the country where the child was habitually resident. This rule will be displaced when an order comes within the terms of the recognition and enforcement provisions of the Brussels IIa Regulation (s 26(2)). Chapter V of the 1986 Act facilitates the almost automatic recognition and enforcement of judgments in intra-UK cases once the procedural steps detailed therein are satisfied.

INTERNATIONAL CHILD ABDUCTION

The formation and subsequent disintegration of "international" families has led to a significant increase in recent times of the wrongful removal and retention of children across international boundaries. The primary legal instrument in this area is the Hague Convention of 25 October 1980 on the Civil Aspects of International Child Abduction, implemented in the United Kingdom by the Child Abduction and Custody Act 1985. The 1980 Hague Convention benefits from a global membership of Contracting States, with its principal aim being the prompt return of children wrongfully removed to or retained in a Contracting State (Art 1). Additionally, when the Contracting States are also EU Member States the Convention is "complemented" by the relevant provisions of the Brussels IIa Regulation (Recital (17)).

Application of the Convention

Before the "prompt return" mechanism of the Convention will be activated it is necessary that the circumstances of the child fall within the scope of the Convention. First, the child concerned must be habitually resident in a Contracting State and have been taken to, or retained in, another Contracting State (Art 4). If return is ultimately ordered then it will be a return to this state of habitual residence. The Convention thus provides an indirect rule of jurisdiction which identifies the courts of the state of the child's habitual residence as the *forum conveniens* for determining any disputes in relation to the child. Article 4 also states that the Convention shall cease to apply when the child attains the age of 16 years and this will be so even if proceedings under the Convention are commenced before the child's 16th birthday (*Re H (Abduction: Child of 16)* (2000)). If the removal or retention of the child is wrongful in terms of Art 3 then, where less than a year has elapsed, between the date of the wrongful removal or retention and the date of the commencement of the proceedings, the child is to be returned forthwith (Art 12(1)). Even if more than one year has elapsed a return should still be ordered (Art 12(2)). However, a return may be resisted if one of the exceptions to return is established (Arts 12(2) and 13).

The concepts of removal and retention

The terms "removal" and "retention" are mutually exclusive. A child will either be removed to, or retained in, a Contracting State and the Convention does not countenance a situation whereby a retention follows an initial removal. A removal occurs where a child is taken across an international frontier without permission, whereas a retention involves a child being taken to a foreign jurisdiction lawfully but then being kept in this jurisdiction beyond the agreed return date. Further, both removal and retention are considered to have occurred on a specific date, with the consequence that a retention is not a continuing state of affairs, it is a single event (*Re H; Re S (Abduction: Custody Rights)* (1991)).

Rights of custody

A removal or retention of a child will only be wrongful when the act is in breach of rights of custody which were actually being exercised at the time of the removal or retention (Art 3). The existence of such rights is to be referred to the law of the Contracting State in which the child was habitually resident immediately before the removal or retention (Art 3(a)). The Convention adopts a permissive approach to rights of custody in seeking to bring the largest possible range of right holders and sources of rights within its scope. Thus, rights of custody may be attributed to a person, an institution or any other body, including a court (*Re H (Abduction: Rights of Custody)* (2000)), and may arise in particular by operation of law or by reason of a judicial or administrative decision, or by reason of an agreement having legal effect under the law of the state of habitual residence.

While reference must be made to the law of the child's state of habitual residence to determine what rights exist in respect of the child, the determination as to whether these rights constitute a right of custody for the purposes of the Convention is to be made in accordance with the autonomous definition found in Art 5(a) that rights of custody include rights relating to the care of the person of the child and, in particular, the right to determine the child's place of residence. A right to determine residence, notably via a power to veto any international relocation, will constitute a right of custody under the Convention, even if this right exists in isolation (*Re D (A Child) (Abduction: Rights of Custody)* (2006)).

It is not sufficient that custody rights merely exist; the applicant must also show that these rights were actually being exercised at the time of the removal or retention (Arts 3(b) and 13(1)(a)). This is not a particularly onerous requirement to fulfil and, in the words of the United States Court of Appeals for the Sixth Circuit, only acts of "clear and unequivocal abandonment" will indicate a failure to exercise rights of custody (*Friedrich* v *Friedrich* (1996)). This approach was approved by the Inner House of the Court of Session in *AJ* v *FJ* (2005).

Exceptions to return

Where an applicant establishes that the removal or retention of a child was wrongful, the court seised in the state of refuge is required to order the return of the child unless it is satisfied that one of the exceptions to return has been established. The availability of these exceptions attempts to balance the principle that it is in the interests of children generally that issues concerning their future should be considered by the authorities in their home state against the necessity that in certain individual cases it will not be in the bests interests of the child to be returned. British courts, particularly the English Court of Appeal, have adopted a restrictive approach to these exceptions. Further, it is important to note that, even if an exception is made out, this simply gives the court the *discretion* not to order a return; in most circumstances it does not *mandate* this course of action.

Consent

The first exception to return is that the person, institution or other body seeking the return had consented to the removal or retention (Art 13(1)(a)). Consent is something that is given before or at the time of the removal and denotes acceptance of the child living in another country, at least for the indefinite future. Consent may be given to a potential future removal as long and this consent remains effective at the time of the actual removal.

While consent must be real, positive and unequivocal this does not mean that it has to be in writing and it may be given orally or even inferred from conduct (*Re K (Abduction: Consent)* (1997)). Even if the court seised does consider the consent exception to be made out, it may still exercise its discretion in favour of returning the child (*Re D (Abduction: Discretionary Return)* (2000)).

Acquiescence

The acquiescence exception is very similar to the consent exception but concerns the actions of the left-behind parent following the removal or retention rather than before or at the time of the occurrence. Acquiescence will be established where that person's words or actions clearly and unequivocally show that the return of the child is not being insisted upon. These words or actions must be wholly inconsistent with a request for the summary return of the child and acquiescence will not be found in attempts at reconciliation, efforts to maintain contact with the child in the requested state, or negotiations to secure a voluntary return. Delay in the issuing of a return petition may be a factor suggestive of acquiescence but the weight of this consideration will be lessened if there is a reasonable explanation for the delay (*H* v *H (Child Abduction: Acquiescence)* (1998)).

Grave risk of harm

Article 13(1)(b) provides that the judicial or administrative authority of the requested state is not bound to order the return of the child if there is a grave risk that the return would expose the child to physical or psychological harm or otherwise place the child in an intolerable situation. As can be deduced from the wording of Art 13(1)(b), this is an exception that will be applicable only in particularly extreme circumstances and it has been interpreted very strictly by the British courts. It is accepted that some disruption and emotional upheaval is inevitable when a return is ordered and such incidental harm will not normally be sufficient to activate Art 13(1)(b). The grave risk must be to the child and any grave risk to the abductor should he or she return to the child's state of habitual residence is not directly relevant. Such risk to a parent will be relevant under Art 13(1)(b) only if it can be shown to cause the child psychological harm, or otherwise place the child in an intolerable situation.

If allegations of risk are raised in return proceedings, the approach of the courts is to consider if the authorities in the state of habitual residence will be able to provide an adequate response to these issues and put measures in place to protect the child. If the foreign authorities will be able to secure the safety of the child then the child will usually be returned and it is only when there is clear evidence to suggest this will not happen that the "grave risk" exception will be upheld (Q, *Petitioner* (2001)). An argument of grave risk premised on the separation of the child from the abductor should the latter refuse to return with the child will usually be insufficient to activate the exception, as the abductor should not be allowed to both create and rely on the harmful situation. Should a grave risk of harm be established then, in contrast to the other exceptions, there is little scope for the exercise of judicial discretion still to order that the child be returned (*Re D (A Child) (Abduction: Rights of Custody)* (2006), per Baroness Hale at [55]).

Objections of the child

Under Art 13(2) a return may also be refused if a child objects to being returned and has attained an age and degree of maturity at which it is appropriate to take account of his views. There is no absolute threshold below which a child will not be considered to have attained such an age and the degree of maturity of the child will be considered on an individual basis (*W* v *W* (2010)). In evaluating the objections of the child the court must be wary that the views of the child may have been influenced by the abductor to an impermissible degree and do not reflect the genuine feelings of the child (*C* v *C* (2008)). While an expression of a preference to stay in one place may be viewed as an objection to going to another, it does not follow automatically that in all cases the expression of a preference amounts to the objection of the alternative (*P* v *S* (2002)). In intra-EU cases, Art 11(2) of the Brussels IIa Regulation requires that the child is given the opportunity to be heard during the proceedings unless this appears inappropriate having regard to his or her age or degree of maturity. Even if the views of the child are expressed, this does not mandate that they be accepted and, even if the views are accepted, the court may still order that the child be returned.

Settlement

The exception contained in Art 12(2) will only become operative once more than a year has elapsed between the commission of the wrongful act and the commencement of the return proceedings. Whether the child is to be considered settled in the requested state requires evidence of more than mere adjustment to the new surroundings. Instead, reference must be made to the physical and emotional attachments made by the child, the level of integration and the stability of the current living arrangements. While a child living in concealment in order to avoid detection may make a finding of settlement more difficult it does not preclude such a finding (*Re C (Abduction: Settlement) (No 2)* (2005)). As with other exceptions, a finding of settlement does not preclude an order for return being made and the court seised may exercise its discretion to return the child notwithstanding such a finding.

Summary return and the ECHR

The emphasis in the Convention on the prompt return of the child to its state of habitual residence has recently been considered by the Grand Chamber of the European Court of Human Rights in the context of Art 8 of the European Convention on Human Rights which guarantees everyone the right to respect for his private and family life. The decision in *Neulinger* v *Switzerland* (2011) caused particular concern due to the very wide pronouncements made by the court (at paras 138 and 139) regarding the need for the requested court to give priority to the best interests of the individual child, to conduct an in-depth examination of the entire family situation and make a balanced and reasonable assessment of the respective interests of each person. While such an approach appears to be in direct contract to the Convention's summary return mechanism, efforts have been made to minimise its effect by both the Supreme Court in *Re E (Children) (Abduction: Custody Appeal)* (2011) and the President of the European Court of Human Rights, speaking in an extra-judicial capacity (as considered by the Supreme Court at para [25]).

Intra-EU child abductions

In cases of child abduction as between EU Member States the provisions of the 1980 Hague Convention must now operate in conjunction with the relevant articles of the Brussels IIa Regulation, primarily Arts 10 and 11. Article 10 regulates jurisdiction in cases of child abduction by providing that, in cases of wrongful removal or retention of the child, the courts of the Member State where the child was habitually resident immediately before the wrongful removal or retention shall retain jurisdiction until the child has acquired a habitual residence in another Member State and one of a number of alternative conditions contained in Art 10 is satisfied.

Article 11(2), as has been considered above, ensures that the child is given the opportunity to be heard during the proceedings, while Art 11(3) requires courts to act expeditiously in child abduction proceedings. Article 11(4) states that a court cannot refuse to return a child on the basis of grave risk if it is established that adequate arrangements have been made to secure the protection of the child after his or her return and therefore reflects the existing practice considered above. Article 11(6), (7) and (8) introduces a review mechanism which operates in conjunction with, and may override, a decision made under the 1980 Hague Convention. Article 11(6) provides that where a non-return order is made on the basis of one of the Art 13 exceptions, notification of this fact shall be given to the authorities in the child's state of habitual residence. Article 11(7) then provides for the court in the state of habitual residence to examine the question of custody of the child. Should the outcome of these proceedings be a judgment which requires the return of the child to that state then, notwithstanding the earlier judgment of non-return under the Convention, this subsequent judgment will automatically be enforceable in all Member States and must be complied with by the courts of the Member State to which the child was removed or in which he was retained in.

Non-Convention cases

Where a child habitually resident in a non-Contracting State is wrongfully removed to, or retained in, Scotland the case will be dealt with under the common law. Although such cases have been influenced by the approach taken under the Convention, they can be distinguished on the basis that priority is to be given to the best interests of the individual child, supported by a more detailed inquiry into the child's situation, and, consequently, less weight will be attached to the principle of summary return (*Re J (A Child) (Custody Rights: Jurisdiction)* (2005)).

ADOPTION

The Adoption and Children (Scotland) Act 2007 establishes a single framework for both domestic and inter-country adoptions which mostly, but not entirely, replaces the previously applicable legislative provisions. Within this framework an important distinction is drawn between Convention adoptions and non-Convention adoptions, the Convention in question being the Hague Convention of 29 May 1993 on Protection of Children and Co-operation in Respect of Intercountry Adoption (implemented in the United Kingdom by the Adoption (Intercountry Aspects) Act 1999). The former category refers to intercountry adoptions involving the United Kingdom and another Contracting State of the 1993 Convention. The latter category of non-Convention, or overseas, adoptions refers to those intercountry adoptions involving a country which is on the United Kingdom's list of designated countries as set out in the Adoption (Designation of Overseas Adoptions) Order 1973 (SI 1973/19). A small number of adoptions do not come within the terms of either of these categories and remain subject to the common law.

Convention adoptions

Part 3 of the Adoptions with a Foreign Element (Scotland) Regulations 2009 (SSI 2009/182) regulates the adoption procedure in Scotland when the United Kingdom is either the receiving state or the state of origin under the 1993 Hague Convention. The former refers to the situation of incoming adoptions where a person or couple habitually resident in the British Islands wishes to adopt a child habitually resident outwith the British Islands (regs 10–37) and the latter refers to the situation of an outgoing adoption where a person or couple habitually resident outwith the British Islands wishes to adopt a child who is habitually resident in the British Islands (regs 38–52).

The Convention itself establishes a detailed procedural framework which aims to control and regulate the manner in which intercountry adoptions between Contracting States may be arranged and completed. The Convention will apply where a child habitually resident in one Contracting State, (the "state of origin"), has been, is being, or is to be moved to another Contracting State (the "receiving state"), either after the adoption in the state of origin by spouses or a person habitually resident in the receiving state, or for the purposes of such an adoption in the receiving state or in the state of origin (Art 2(1)). The material scope of the Convention is limited to adoptions which create a permanent parent–child relationship (Art 2(2)), even if the adoption does not completely extinguish all previous parent–child relationships, and which involve children under 18 (Art 3). Articles 4 and 5 then provide an extensive list of requirements that must be satisfied by the authorities in both the state of origin (Art 4) and the receiving state (Art 5) before an adoption within the scope of the Convention will be permitted. These requirements include such issues as the authorities in the state of origin having given due consideration to the possibilities for placement of the child in the state of origin (Art 4(b)) and, as regards the authorities in the receiving state, it having been determined that the child is or will be authorised to enter and reside permanently in the receiving state (Art 5(c)).

Chapter IV of the Convention details the procedural requirements of intercountry adoptions which are implemented in Scotland by the Adoptions with a Foreign Element (Scotland) Regulations 2009 (SSI 2009/182). Article 14 provides that persons habitually resident in a Contracting State, who wish to adopt a child habitually resident in another Contracting State, shall apply to the Central Authority in the state of their habitual residence. This prerequisite is augmented in Scotland so as to require habitual residence in a part of the British Islands for a period of not less than a year ending with the date of application (2009 Regulations, reg 12(1)(b)).

Articles 15–22 then detail the roles and responsibilities of the Central Authorities in both the state of origin and the receiving state.

Chapter V of the Convention clarifies the recognition to be given to, and the effects of, an adoption granted in one Contracting State in all other Contracting States. Under Art 23, an adoption certified by the competent authority in the state of the adoption, whether this be the state of origin or the receiving state, as having been made in accordance with the Convention shall be recognised by operation of law in the other Contracting States. The recognition of an adoption may be refused in a Contracting State only if the adoption is manifestly contrary to its public policy, taking into account the best interests of the child (Art 24). Articles 26 and 27 detail the legal consequences which will flow from the recognition of a Convention adoption.

Non-Convention adoptions

Non-Convention, or overseas, adoptions are those adoptions to or from a country which is on the United Kingdom's list of designated countries as set out in the Adoption (Designation of Overseas Adoptions) Order 1973 (SI 1973/19). The requirements for non-Convention cases are set out in Pt I, Ch 6 of the Adoption and Children (Scotland) Act 2007 which, like the procedural requirements applicable to Convention adoptions, places restrictions on both incoming and outgoing adoptions. Further requirements are to be found in the Adoptions with a Foreign Element (Scotland) Regulations 2009 (SSI 2009/182), Pt 2. Such overseas adoptions will be recognised automatically in Scotland as if the adoption order had been made in Scotland. The Court of Session may, however, find that such an adoption is no longer valid in Great Britain, on the ground that the adoption is contrary to public policy or that the authority which purported to authorise the adoption was not competent (2007 Act, s 68(2)).

Adoption orders at common law

Where an adoption does not come within the scope of either the Convention or the statutory regime then recognition must be sought under the common-law rules. Such an adoption is likely to be recognised only if the adoptive parents are domiciled in the state of origin and, even if this requirement is satisfied, recognition may still be refused on grounds of public policy (*Re Valentine's Settlement* (1965)).

Essential Facts

Status
- The concepts of legitimacy and illegitimacy are no longer relevant to the determination of status under Scots law but may still be relevant when a person's status falls to be determined according to some other law.

Parental responsibility
- There are three distinct jurisdictional regimes relating to matters of parental responsibility: (1) the Brussels IIa Regulation; (2) the 1996 Hague Convention; and (3) the Family Law Act 1986.
- Chapter II, section 2 of the Brussels IIa Regulation governs jurisdiction in matters of parental responsibility and identifies the habitual residence of the child as the principal ground of jurisdiction.
- Chapter II of the 1996 Hague Convention governs jurisdiction when a child is habitually resident in a non-EU Contracting State and contains provisions that are similar, but not identical, to those contained in the Brussels IIa Regulation.
- Cases that fall outside the scope of both the Brussels IIa Regulation and the 1996 Hague Convention will be governed by Ch III of the Family Law Act 1986.
- Chapter III of the 1996 Hague Convention identifies the applicable law in matters of parental responsibility and these rules are also applicable when jurisdiction is taken under the Regulation.
- Chapter III of the Brussels IIa Regulation facilitates the mutual recognition of judgments between Member States. Corresponding rules of recognition and enforcement are found in Ch IV of the 1996 Hague Convention and Ch V of the 1986 Act.

International child abduction
- The principal aim of the 1980 Hague Convention is to ensure that a child wrongfully removed to, or retained in, one Contracting State is returned promptly to the Contracting State in which he is habitually resident.
- A return may be refused if it can be shown that the rights of custody were not being exercised at the time of the removal or retention; that the removal or retention had been consented to or subsequently acquiesced in; that the return would subject the child to a grave risk of harm; that the child objects to the return; or that the child is now settled in his new environment.

- In cases of child abduction as between EU Member States the 1980 Hague Convention operates in conjunction with the Brussels IIa Regulation. In particular, Art 11(6), (7) and (8) of the Regulation introduce a review mechanism which may override a non-return order made under the 1980 Hague Convention.

Adoption
- The Adoption and Children (Scotland) Act 2007 establishes a single framework for both domestic and inter-country adoptions, with a distinction being drawn between Convention adoptions and non-Convention adoptions.
- Convention adoptions are those governed by the Hague Convention of 29 May 1993 on Protection of Children and Co-operation in Respect of Intercountry Adoption.
- Non-Convention, or overseas, adoptions are those adoptions to or from a country which is on the United Kingdom's list of designated countries as set out in the Adoption (Designation of Overseas Adoptions) Order 1973 (SI 1973/19).

Essential Cases

Proceedings Brought by A (2010): the factors relevant in the identification of habitual residence under the Brussels IIa Regulation in matters of parental responsibility include, but are not limited to, the duration, regularity, conditions and reasons for the stay in a Member State and the family's move to that state, the child's nationality, the place and conditions of attendance at school, linguistic knowledge, and the family and social relationships of the child in that state.

Re D (A Child) (Abduction: Rights of Custody) (2006): the concept of a right of custody is given an autonomous definition under the 1980 Hague Convention independent of national classifications. In particular, a right to determine residence, notably via a power to veto any international relocation, will constitute a right of custody under the Convention, even if this right exists in isolation.

Q, Petitioner (2001): a return was refused under Art 13(1)(b) (grave risk) of the 1980 Hague Convention as the Scottish court was not convinced that the French authorities would be able to provide two children with adequate protection.

Neulinger v Switzerland (2011): decision of the Grand Chamber of the European Court of Human Rights which considers the operation of the 1980 Hague Convention in light of Art 8 of the European Convention on Human Rights which guarantees everyone the right to respect for his private and family life.

12 PROPERTY

The distinction between moveable and immoveable property is fundamental to the private international law of Scotland and this classification
will be made in accordance with the rules of the *lex situs*, the law of the
country in which the property is situated (*Macdonald* v *Macdonald* (1932)).
This classification will be followed even if it leads to a different result to that
which would apply in a purely domestic context. As will be seen below,
nearly every question relating to immoveable property will be referred to
the *lex situs*, while questions relating to moveable property may be referred
to one or more of a number of different laws.

IMMOVEABLE PROPERTY

The rule that questions relating to immoveable property are governed by
the *lex situs* is premised on the principle that the law of the country in
which the property is situated will have the strongest connection to the
property. This principle is reflected in international instruments, with the
Brussels I Regulation providing that the courts of the Member State in
which immoveable property is situated will have exclusive jurisdiction in
proceedings which have as their object rights *in rem* in that property or a
tenancy of that property (Art 22(1)). Further, Art 4(1)(c) of the Rome I
Regulation (Art 4(3) of the 1980 Rome Convention) provides that, in
the absence of choice, a contract relating to a right *in rem* in immoveable
property or to a tenancy of immoveable property will be governed by the
law of the country where the property is situated.

Capacity

Capacity and the power to transact in relation to immoveable property are
governed by the *lex situs*.

Contracts

A distinction should be drawn between contractual obligations relating to
immoveable property and the actual transfer/conveyance of a right *in rem*
in immoveable property. In relation to the former, formal validity will be
governed by Art 11 of the Rome I Regulation (Art 9 of the Convention)
as regards those contractual obligations which come within the scope of
the instrument. Article 11(1) provides that a contract concluded between

persons who, or whose agents, are in the same country at the time of its conclusion is formally valid if it satisfies the formal requirements of the law which governs it in substance under the Regulation, or of the law of the country where it is concluded. However, where the subject-matter of the contract is a right *in rem* in immoveable property or a tenancy of immoveable property, Art 11(1) is buttressed by Art 11(5) (Art 9(6) of the Convention) which provides that the contract will be subject to the requirements of form of the law of the country where the property is situated if by that law those requirements are imposed, irrespective of the country where the contract is concluded and irrespective of the law governing the contract, and those requirements cannot be derogated from by agreement. Under the common law a distinction is made between an obligation to convey and the conveyance itself and a contract relating to immoveable property in Scotland will satisfy the requirements of formal validity if it complies with either the *lex situs* or the *lex loci actus* (*Hamilton v Wakefield* (1993)).

Under the Rome I Regulation the essential validity of a contract relating to immoveable property will be determined according to the applicable law identified elsewhere in the Regulation (Art 10(1)), subject to the exception contained in Art 10(2) (with the equivalent provisions found in Art 8 of the Convention). If the dispute is before a court in Scotland then the applicable law will be subject to the overriding mandatory provisions of the forum (Art 9 of the Regulation; Art 7 of the Convention). As the applicable law, whether it be chosen by the parties under Art 3 or determined in the absence of choice under Art 4(1)(c), is likely to be the *lex situs* of the property, this law will usually determine matters of essential validity. The same law would also be applicable to matters of essential validity under the common law.

Proprietary rights

The existence and nature of real rights in land or other immoveables are governed by the *lex situs*. This rule applies to all property regarded as immoveable according to the *lex situs*. All deeds of title must comply with the *lex situs* in matters of both form and essentials.

MOVEABLE PROPERTY

The category of moveable property can be further subdivided into corporeal moveables (such as motor vehicles), and incorporeal moveables (such as money debts). Different rules apply depending on into which sub-category the property in question falls.

Corporeal moveables

Historically, the law applicable to corporeal moveables was considered to be the law of the domicile of the owner of the property in question. While this law may still be applicable in certain circumstances, it is now possible that another law, such as the *lex situs*, will be applicable. The universality that may have existed in the past is now no longer apparent and no single system of law has a claim to govern every question relating to the transfer of corporeal moveables.

As a general rule, proprietary rights in corporeal moveable property are governed by the *lex situs*. The consequence of this rule is that, following a transfer of corporeal moveable property situated abroad, any proprietary rights conferred on the transferee will be recognised in Scotland if the transfer was validly effected in accordance with the *lex situs*. Conversely, a real right to moveable property in Scotland does not pass by virtue of transactions effected abroad until these have been intimated to the custodian in Scotland.

A further distinction exists between questions of personal liability affecting the parties to a contract to transfer moveable property and the matter of a real right to the property itself. Under this distinction, the questions in relation to the former will be referred to the applicable law of the contract while questions as regards the latter will be a matter for the *lex situs* (*North-Eastern Bank* v *Poynter & Co* (1894) and *Inglis* v *Robertson* (1898)).

Difficulties arise when matters of contract law and property law intersect in the context of retention of title clauses. Such clauses generally provide that goods delivered by the seller to the buyer remain the property of the former until the goods have been paid for in full. Where both the contract and the property are subject to the same applicable law then this will cause few issues but problems can develop when the applicable law of the contract differs from the *lex situs* of the goods. In such circumstances there is no clear answer on the question as to whether a clause acceptable by the governing law of the contract of which it forms part will be regarded as invalid if it is not also recognised as valid under the *lex situs* of the property at the time at which the contract is entered into.

Incorporeal moveables

The category of incorporeal moveables signifies those proprietary rights which have no physical existence, such as debts, shares and securities or funds in bank accounts. As these rights have no physical location, an artificial *situs* must be identified for the purposes of classification, with, for example, a money debt being situated at the place where the debtor resides. There are a number of different laws which may be applicable to the assignation of an incorporeal right, namely: the *lex domicilii* of either the creditor or the debtor; the *lex loci actus*; or the *lex situs*. Incorporeal moveables are of several different classes and the same conflicts rules may not be applicable in each case.

Article 14 of the Rome I Regulation (Art 12 of the 1980 Rome Convention) may also be applicable to certain assignations, subject to the exclusions contained in Art 1(2). If the Regulation is engaged, Art 14 will apply to not only the contractual aspects of the assignation but also the proprietary aspects (Recital (38)). Article 14(1) provides that the relationship between assignor and assignee under a voluntary assignation or contractual subrogation of a claim against another person (the debtor) shall be governed by the law that applies to the contract between the assignor and assignee under the Regulation, ie as chosen under Art 3 or identified in the absence of choice under Art 4. Article 14(2) states that the law governing the assigned or subrogated claim shall determine its assignability; the relationship between the assignee and the debtor; the conditions under which the assignment or subrogation can be invoked against the debtor; and whether the debtor's obligations have been discharged. Article 14(3) defines "assignment" as including outright transfers of claims, transfers of claims by way of security and pledges or other security rights over claims.

Essential Facts

- There is a fundamental distinction between moveable and immoveable property, with this classification being made according to the rules of the *lex situs*.
- Matters relating to immoveable property will in general be referred to the *lex situs*.
- Moveable property can be subdivided further into corporeal moveables and incorporeal moveables.

13 SUCCESSION

It is now increasingly likely that a person domiciled in Scotland will acquire property situated in another country or, conversely, that persons domiciled outside Scotland will own property situated within Scotland. Upon death, the devolution of such an international estate raises key questions of private international law, particularly with regard to the identification of the appropriate law to govern the distribution of the deceased's estate. This chapter will consider the rules of private international law applicable to both testate and intestate succession, focusing principally on issues of choice of law and beginning with a brief overview of the rules applicable to the administration of estates.

ADMINISTRATION OF ESTATES

No person is entitled to take any administrative act in the estate of a deceased person who has left property in Scotland until he has obtained the authority of the court. In Scotland, this is known as confirmation – a process whereby executors are judicially recognised in their office and receive a title to the property and assets of a deceased person. Once confirmed, the executor is entrusted with the task of administering the estate in order to ensure that all debts are satisfied and that the net surplus of the estate is distributed to the appropriate heirs. Confirmation is dependent on the existence of property in Scotland and if the deceased left no such property then confirmation will not be granted, even if the deceased died domiciled in Scotland. Conversely, if a deceased person leaves property in Scotland, his executors may obtain confirmation in the Scottish courts even though the person died domiciled elsewhere.

Under ss 1 and 2 of the Administration of Estates Act 1971, a Scottish confirmation will, if granted in respect of an estate of a person who died domiciled in Scotland, be treated for the purposes of the law of England and Wales and Northern Ireland as if it had been granted under the equivalent procedures in place in those jurisdictions. A reciprocal provision is found in s 3 to ensure that grants from England and Wales or Northern Ireland will be of the like force and effect and have the same operation in relation to property in Scotland as a Scottish confirmation. Accordingly, where a person dies domiciled in Scotland, the granting of confirmation in

Scotland will be recognised throughout the entire United Kingdom and be effective in relation to all property situated therein.

Where a person dies domiciled outside the United Kingdom, the Scottish courts will follow the law of the deceased's domicile and grant confirmation to the person entrusted with the administration of the estate under that law in relation to property situated in Scotland. If such a person is yet to be appointed in the country of the domicile of the deceased, confirmation will be granted to the person who would be entitled under that law to administer the estate of the deceased. If the deceased is domiciled in a country which does not provide for a process analogous to confirmation, confirmation will be given to the person entitled to administer the estate by the law of the domicile. If a person domiciled overseas nominates an executor in his will, this person will be confirmed in relation to property situated in Scotland if the will is valid according to the law of the deceased's domicile.

Special provisions exist for the "resealing" of grants of representation, corresponding to a Scottish confirmation, made in those countries identified under the Colonial Probates Act 1892 and the Colonial Probates (Protected States and Mandated Territories) Act 1927. Once resealed in Scotland, grants from those countries specified will have the like force and effect and the same operation as if it were a confirmation granted by the Scottish court. Reciprocal provisions exist for the resealing of Scottish confirmations in the identified countries.

MATTERS RELEVANT TO BOTH INTESTATE AND TESTATE SUCCESSION

The scission principle

Fundamental to the Scottish choice of law rules governing succession, whether testate or intestate, is what is known as the "scission principle". Under this principle a distinction is drawn between succession to moveables (referred to the law of the domicile of the deceased), and succession to immoveables (referred to the *lex situs*, the law of the country in which the property is situated). The approach of Scots law (and the law of England and Wales) can be compared with the approach taken in other jurisdictions which have rejected the scission principle in favour of a single governing law applicable to the entirety of the deceased's estate.

Legal rights

Legal rights may be claimed under both intestate and testate succession and provide a surviving spouse (*jus relicti/jus relictae*) or civil partner (Civil

Partnership Act 2004, s 131) and/or issue (*legitim*) a right to a share in the estate of the deceased that cannot be defeated by testamentary provision. Thus, where a person dies survived by a spouse or civil partner then, if there are no issue, that person is entitled to one-half of the moveable net estate belonging to the deceased at the time of death. If the deceased is also survived by issue, the surviving spouse or civil partner has a right to one-third of that moveable net estate. Similarly, the surviving issue of the deceased have a right to one-half of the moveable net estate belonging to the deceased at the time of death if there is no surviving spouse or civil partner, and a right to one-third if there is such a survivor. Due to such rights being limited to the moveable estate of the deceased, such rights may, by definition, be claimed only when the deceased died domiciled in Scotland.

INTESTATE SUCCESSION

Immoveable property

It is a well-established rule that all questions of intestate succession to immoveables are governed by the *lex situs*. This law will determine both whether the property is immoveable and whether it has fallen into intestacy and, if so, it will be determinative in identifying the person to whom the property is to descend.

Moveable property

It is equally well settled that intestate succession to moveable estate is governed by the law of the deceased's domicile at the date of his death, wherever that property may be situated.

Prior rights

Prior rights were established by the Succession (Scotland) Act 1964 and are available in circumstances of total or partial intestacy. Prior rights are not exercisable in circumstances where the deceased has disposed of his entire estate by testamentary disposition. Section 8 of the 1964 Act confers on the surviving spouse or civil partner of an intestate an interest in a qualifying dwellinghouse where that interest does not exceed £473,000. As the dwellinghouse will be classified as immoveable property, governed therefore by the *lex situs*, this prior right will be applicable to all qualifying dwellinghouses in Scotland, irrespective of the domicile of the deceased at his date of death. Conversely, this prior right will not be exercisable against a dwellinghouse situated outside Scotland, even if the deceased died domiciled in Scotland. Where the value of the dwellinghouse exceeds £473,000, the survivor is entitled to receive a sum of money in lieu of the house. Although *prima facie* a right in moveable property, this right to a sum of money in lieu of the dwellinghouse will be treated as immoveable property and therefore governed by Scots law – the *lex situs*.

Where a person dies intestate leaving a spouse or civil partner, and the intestate estate includes the furniture and plenishings of a dwellinghouse, s 8(3) provides that the surviving spouse or civil partner shall receive a prior right in such furniture and plenishings to a maximum value of £29,000. This prior right is an interest in moveable property and available only when the deceased died domiciled in Scotland.

Section 9 entitles the surviving spouse or civil partner to a prior right to financial provision on intestacy, the value of which depends on whether or not the intestate was survived by issue. Although *prima facie* moveable, this right is to be "borne by, and paid out of, the parts of the intestate estate consisting of heritable and moveable property respectively" (s 9(3)). Consequently, where the deceased dies domiciled in Scotland, this sum will be paid out of his moveable estate wherever situated and his immoveable estate in Scotland. If the deceased is domiciled outside Scotland then the charge will be operative against only that immoveable estate situated in Scotland.

Cohabitants

Section 29 of the Family Law (Scotland) Act 2006 provides that a surviving cohabitant may make an application to the court for a payment out of the deceased's net intestate estate of a capital sum, and for the transfer of such property (whether heritable or moveable) from that estate. An application under s 29 may be made only when the deceased was domiciled in Scotland immediately before his death (s 29(1)(b)(i)) and with regard to heritable property, only in relation to such property situated in Scotland (*Kerr* v *Mangan* (2014)).

TESTATE SUCCESSION

Capacity

Personal capacity is concerned with the effect factors such as age, facility and circumvention or undue influence may have upon a testator's ability to create a valid will. These issues will be governed by the law of the testator's domicile as regards moveables. Where a testator's domicile changes as between the date of execution of the will and the date of death, the domicile apparent at the earlier date should govern such issues. Questions of personal capacity relating to immoveables will be referred to the *lex situs*.

Formal validity

Whether a will is properly executed in matters of form will be governed by the law identified under the Wills Act 1963. This Act implements the provisions of the Hague Convention of 5 October 1961 on the Conflicts of Laws Relating to the Form of Testamentary Dispositions and provides a permissive system under which questions of formal validity may be referred to a number of different laws. Accordingly, s 1 provides that a will shall be treated as properly executed if its execution conformed to the internal law in force in the territory where it was executed, or in the territory where, at the time of its execution or of the testator's death, he was domiciled or had his habitual residence, or in a state of which, at either of those times, he was a national. This section applies to wills concerning both moveables and immoveables but, in relation to the latter, s 2(1)(b) provides that, in addition to those laws identified under s 1(1), a will, so far as it disposes of immoveable property, will be treated as properly executed if its execution conformed to the internal law in force in the territory where the property is situated. Section 2(1)(a) provides an additional rule of closest connection with regard to wills executed on board a vessel or aircraft.

Essential validity

Essential validity is concerned with all matters pertaining to the validity and enforceability of the provisions of a will, such as whether a testator can completely disinherit his spouse or children. These matters are sometimes referred to as the "proprietary capacity" of the testator. The essential validity of testamentary dispositions will be governed by the law of the deceased's last domicile as regards moveables and by the *lex situs* as regards immoveables.

Construction

A will is to be construed according to the law intended by the testator. A testator may expressly choose the law by which his will should be construed but this choice will be given effect only insofar as it is consistent with the law of his domicile. Where the intention of the testator is uncertain there is a presumption that a will of moveable estate falls to be construed in accordance with the law of the domicile of the testator, and a will of immoveable estate will probably also be construed according to the same law (*Mitchell and Baxter* v *Davies* (1875)). These are, however, only presumptions and may be rebutted by evidence that the testator intended a different law to govern matters of construction (*Dellar* v *Zivy* (2007)). The reference to the testator's domicile as regards moveable estate is a reference to the domicile of the testator at the time the will is made, not domicile at the time of death.

This interpretation is consistent with the terms of s 4 of the Wills Act 1963 which provides that the construction of a will shall not be altered by reason of any change in the testator's domicile after the execution of the will.

Revocation

A later will may revoke an earlier will either expressly or by implication. A revocation will be operative only if the original instrument is capable of revocation and the testator has capacity to revoke under the law of his domicile at the time of the alleged revocation (*Sawrey-Cookson* v *Sawrey-Cookson's Trustees* (1905)). The validity and construction of the later instrument will be subject to the rules discussed above, with an additional rule as regards formal validity available under s 2(1)(c) of the Wills Act 1963 to the effect that a deed of revocation will be treated as properly executed if it satisfies the terms of s 1 or if it conforms to the formalities of any system by reference to which the revoked will would be treated as properly executed. The *lex situs* may also be relevant where the disposition is one of immoveable property.

A will disposing of moveables may also be revoked by operation of law, with the question of whether the will is actually revoked being referred to the law of the testator's domicile at the time of the alleged revocation and not at the time of death. For example, the English rule that a marriage revokes any previous will has effect only if the testator is domiciled in England immediately after the marriage (compare *Re Martin* (1900) with *In the Estate of Groos* (1904)). An identical approach is taken in Scotland to the *conditio si testator sine liberis decesserit*, with an earlier will being revoked only if the testator is domiciled in Scotland at the time at which the child is born.

FUTURE DEVELOPMENTS

Domestically, the Scottish Law Commission's 2009 Report on Succession (Scot Law Com No 215) recommends a number of changes to the current law of succession, with Pt 5 of the Report dealing specifically with issues of private international law. These recommendations are yet to be implemented. At the European level, Regulation (EU) No 650/2012 of the European Parliament and of the Council of 4 July 2012 on jurisdiction, applicable law, recognition and enforcement of decisions and acceptance and enforcement of authentic instruments in matters of succession and on the creation of a European Certificate of Succession will apply to the estates of individuals dying on or after 17 August 2015 (Art 83(1)). The United Kingdom, along with Ireland and Denmark, has decided not to opt into this Regulation.

TRUSTS

The private international law aspects of trusts are now governed principally by the Recognition of Trusts Act 1987 which gives effect to the Hague Convention of 1 July 1985 on the Law Applicable to Trusts and on their Recognition. The common law retains a residual role. While Art 22 of the Convention provides that the Convention applies to trusts regardless of the date on which they were created, s 1(5) of the 1987 Act limits the temporal applicability of the Convention to trusts created after the coming into force of the Act, or to acts or omissions occurring after the coming into force of the Act even if the trust was created before this date. Further, and in contrast to the terms of Art 24, s 1(2) applies the rules of the Convention not only to overseas trusts but also to trusts arising under the law of another part of the United Kingdom. Finally, the application of the Convention is not limited to the recognition of trusts arising under the law of a Contracting State and, instead, the United Kingdom applies the terms of the Convention generally, whether or not the trust arises under the law of a Contracting State. The Convention, therefore, is applied universally, both inside and outside the United Kingdom, to conflicts of law in matters relating to trusts.

Article 2 of the Convention defines the meaning of the term "trust" for the purposes of the Convention, with this definition being drawn very broadly in order to accommodate the divergent understanding of trusts under different legal systems. If the trust does come within the terms of Art 2 then Ch II provides rules as to the applicable law. Article 6 states the primary rule that a trust will be governed by the law chosen by the settlor, whether expressly or by implication. In the absence of choice, or in light of an ineffective choice, Art 7 provides that a trust shall be governed by the law with which it is most closely connected and details a non-exhaustive list of factors relevant in this determination. Article 5 states that the Convention does not apply to the extent that the law specified by Ch II does not provide for trusts or the category of trusts involved. Should Art 5 be operative then recourse must be made to the common law. The law specified under either Art 6 or Art 7 will govern the validity of the trust, its construction, its effects, and the administration of the trust and Art 8(2) provides further specification as regards the matters that this law will govern.

The recognition of trusts is facilitated by Ch III, Art 11(1) of which states that a trust created in accordance with the law specified in Ch II will be recognised as a trust. This basic statement is given more context in Art 11(2) where it is explained that recognition implies, as a minimum, that the trust property constitutes a separate fund; that the trustee may sue and be sued in his capacity as trustee; and that he may appear or act in this capacity before a notary or any person acting in an official capacity. Article 11(3) provides further detail as to what the recognition of a trust will imply in light of the applicable law. Article 11 operates subject to the rules contained in Ch IV.

Essential Facts

- Under the scission principle, questions regarding succession to moveables will be referred to the law of the deceased's domicile, while succession to immoveables will be governed by the law of the country in which the property is situated.
- Legal rights may be claimed only when the deceased died domiciled in Scotland.

Intestate succession

- The prior right of a surviving spouse or civil partner on intestacy in a dwellinghouse under s 8 of the Succession (Scotland) Act 1964 is available whenever the property is situated in Scotland, regardless of the domicile of the deceased.
- The prior right in the furniture and plenishings of a dwellinghouse (s 8(3)) will be available only when the deceased dies domiciled in Scotland.
- The prior right to financial provision on intestacy under s 9 will be paid out of both moveables and immoveables when the deceased died domiciled in Scotland but only out of the immoveable estate situated in Scotland if the deceased died domiciled elsewhere.
- An application under s 29 of the Family Law (Scotland) Act 2006 by a surviving cohabitant for provision on intestacy may only be made when the deceased died domiciled in Scotland.

Testate Succession

- Capacity will be governed by the *lex domicilii* as regards moveables and the *lex situs* in relation to immoveables.
- Whether a will is properly executed in matters of form will be governed by the law identified under the Wills Act 1963.
- Essential validity will be governed by the law of the deceased's last domicile as regards moveables and by the *lex situs* as regards immoveables.

Trusts

- The private international law aspects of trusts are governed principally by the Recognition of Trusts Act 1987 which gives effect to the Hague Convention of 1 July 1985 on the Law Applicable to Trusts and on their Recognition.

Essential Cases

Dellar v Zivy (2007): a will is to be interpreted in accordance with the law intended by a testator. In the absence of indications to the contrary, this law is presumed to be the law of the testator's domicile at the time the will was made. This presumption may be rebutted by evidence that the testator intended his will to be interpreted according to the law of some other country.

Sawrey-Cookson v Sawrey-Cookson's Trustees (1905): a revocation will be effective only if the original instrument is capable of revocation and the testator has capacity to revoke under the law of his domicile at the time of the revocation.

INDEX